getting students
to show up

Practical Ideas for Any Outreach Event — from 10 to 10,000
Jonathan McKee

Foreword by Kurt Johnston

ZONDERVAN®

ZONDERVAN.com/
AUTHORTRACKER
follow your favorite authors

"Jonathan always knows how to come with the right amount of inspiration, humor, and information. This is a practical 'what to do' and 'why to do it' book that you'll be able to use over and over as you develop your youth ministry program. I highly recommend *Getting Students to Show Up*."

—Fred Lynch, author and speaker

"I believe this book can help shape and inspire the future of youth ministry evangelism. Jonathan isn't afraid to ask the hard, uncomfortable questions and doesn't ignore the elephants in the room we normally ignore. But despite the uncomfortable realities he raises, Jonathan gives practical advice and, most of all, hope for the gospel being communicated to youth."

—Dan Kimball, author of *The Emerging Church* and *They Like Jesus but Not the Church*

"There's no fluff here and no philosophical rambling, just focused and specific advice every youth worker needs. McKee shows readers how to program their outreach events, whether large or small, from the time the idea is first sparked at a leadership meeting until the lights go down and the last kid leaves the building—on time! *Getting Students to Show Up* is just what today's youth worker needs: No gimmicks or gags, just practical how-tos that have already been tried and found to be true."

—Tamara Rice, media editor, OUTREACH Magazine

"Jonathan McKee is one of the most dynamic communicators in the country when it comes to creating great outreach events. This book is extremely practical and very helpful."

—Jim Burns, Ph.D., president, HomeWord; author of *Creating an Intimate Marriage*

"Finally, a hands-on resource that does a masterful job of laying out a biblical philosophy of outreach and combining it with really practical programming ideas. If you're a youth leader who wants students to show up, then by all means you need *Getting Students to Show Up*."

—Lane Palmer, youth ministry resource director, Dare 2 Share Ministries, Intl.

"Big 'ups' to Jonathan for his insightful and useful book! I can imagine him walking through the youth ministry resource aisle looking for what is *not* there and then delivering to us exactly what we need. Jonathan's ministry experience, vision, and passion to reach non-connected and non-Christian kids truly comes out in this book. His enthusiasm and practical ideas will be useful to any youth worker, church, or parachurch looking to extend the reach of ministry."

—Don Talley, senior director, YFC/USA National Ministries

"I had a conversation with a youth pastor recently who told me that he had given up trying to reach non-churched teenagers. "Today's kids are turned off by the church," he said, "and besides, we can't compete with the entertainment industry." I mumbled something to him about keeping his chin up and/or getting some career counseling. But now I wish I could have handed him a copy of this book. I know it would have changed his mind by the time he reached chapter four. Jon McKee has given us a wonderful resource that will ultimately result in thousands more kids coming to know Christ."

—Wayne Rice, Co-founder of Youth Specialties & Founder of Understanding Your Teenager seminars

Youth Specialties

Getting Students to Show Up: Practical ideas for Any Outreach Event—from 10 to 10,000
Copyright © 2007 by Jonathan McKee

Youth Specialties products, 300 S. Pierce St., El Cajon, CA 92020 are published by
Zondervan, 5300 Patterson Ave. SE, Grand Rapids, MI 49530.

Library of Congress Cataloging-in-Publication Data

McKee, Jonathan R. (Jonathan Ray), 1970-
  Getting students to show up : practical ideas for any outreach event—
from 10 to 10,000 / Jonathan McKee.
    p. cm.
  ISBN-10: 0-310-27216-5 (pbk.)
  ISBN-13: 978-0-310-27216-8 (pbk.)
  1. Church work with teenagers. 2. Church work with students. 3.
Evangelistic work. 4. Non-church-affiliated people. I. Title.
  BV4447.M2377 2007
  259'.23—dc22

                                                                2007006912

---

*Creative Team: Dave Urbanski, SharpSeven Design, Laura Gross, Janie Wilkerson, and
Heather Haggerty
Cover Design by Burnkit*

Printed in the United States of America

---

07 08 09 10 11 12 • 23 22 21 20 19 18 17 16 15 14 13 12 11 10 9 8 7 6 5 4 3 2 1

ACKNOWLEDGMENTS

I thank God for being a solid foundation for an otherwise weak building. God somehow takes all of my mistakes and turns them into something good. It's only through these learning experiences, combined with his strength, that I've ever accomplished anything in my ministry. My work for him is never useless because he never lets it go to waste (1 Corinthians 15:58). It's with this confidence that I continue reaching out to the lost.

Even though my name is on the cover of this book, several others have helped me along the way. In the early stages of this book, eight people reviewed the manuscript, asked questions, added elements I'd missed, and helped me chisel this book into a more effective tool for helping youth workers with outreach programming. This group is made up of volunteer and paid, large group and small group, church and parachurch, big town and little town—and all of them have made a huge impact in the lives of kids around the world. Not only are these eight people my friends, but they're also my "dream team":

Les Christie—William Jessup University

Danette Matty—The Source for Youth Ministry

Rob Maxey—Youth for Christ Sacramento

Tom McKee, Sr.—Advantage Point Systems, Inc.

Lane Palmer—Dare 2 Share Ministries

Scott Rubin—Willow Creek Community Church

K.J. Stephens—Bayside Covenant Church

Don Talley—Campus Life National Office

In addition to these, I must thank my wife, Lori. Not only did she put up with me while I wrote this book, but she also proofed the manuscript several times and helped me immensely with the editing process. Thanks, kiddo!

FOREWORD

Beyond the Three-Cushion Couch

I like movies. I like movies a lot. But I don't like watching movies in a crowded theater. People have a tendency to mess up the movie experience—especially teenagers. I absolutely hate seeing a movie in a theater full of teenagers. More about that later.

When I was in junior high, I attended a tiny church. My junior high youth group consisted of three people. The whole junior high department fit perfectly on a three-cushion couch. We never did outreach. I don't think we ever thought about outreach. In fact, I'm not sure our volunteer youth director even knew outreach was allowed. In hindsight it was probably a good thing. Because if we'd actually reached out, our ministry might have grown from three to four—and one of us would have lost a place on that couch.

When I was in high school, I was invited to a summer beach camp hosted by a church across town. They had a youth ministry of several hundred students—lots of three-cushion couches!—and they understood outreach. The youth pastor talked about it, provided opportunities for it to happen, and modeled it through his lifestyle. In fact, it was through this youth ministry that God grabbed hold of my heart.

Because of my own experience in youth group as a teenager, I find myself in an interesting place when it comes to the topic of outreach. On one hand, I view it as an essential part of every youth group. After all, I'm the result of a youth group that aggressively reached out to unchurched kids. But on the other hand, I'm not super worried about it. My most formative teenage years were spent sitting on a three-cushion couch under the leadership of a volunteer youth worker who didn't know a thing about outreach. Yet, his genuine interest in me and his willingness to be a part of my life planted seeds that the outreach-oriented youth group would harvest later on.

Now back to the movies. When I head to the movie theater on a Friday night and see a crowd of skating, smoking, sarcastic, and sexually charged teenagers hanging around, the first thing that comes to mind is: *I sure hope all of these students aren't seeing the same movie I'm seeing because they're going to totally ruin it for me.* When Jonathan McKee heads to the movies and sees that same crowd of students, the first thing that comes to *his* mind is: *How can we bring the good news of Jesus Christ to these kids?*

Jonathan is passionate about evangelism; it leaks out of him and flows into every arena of his life. When Jonathan starts talking about non-Christian kids, the tone of his voice changes, he gets that look in his eyes, he leans forward in his chair, and he starts moving his arms a lot. Frankly, it's kinda weird. (Don't get me wrong; I like talking about how to reach more kids, but I also like talking about socks.)

As you read this book, keep a pen handy. Make notes in the margins, jot down the questions that pop into your head, and write down the ideas that come to mind. This book will make you think—it sure made me think. You won't be able to implement every idea in your particular ministry setting either, and that's okay too. When you finish reading, you won't have three simple steps for reaching more students—outreach isn't that easy. Reaching the students in your community takes strategy, time, creativity, patience, persistence, and faith. There really aren't any shortcuts. This book is a starting point, not the end-all.

Maybe what I like most about *Getting Students to Show Up* is the fact that it wasn't written in isolation by some guy with a bunch of unproven and theoretical outreach ideas. What you hold in your hands is a labor of love written by a man who is good at it, who gets it, and who is, most importantly, passionate about it.

Read, think, strategize, pray, and take a few steps. Who knows, maybe someday you'll need to buy an extra couch for your youth room.

—*Kurt Johnston*

CONTENTS

where it all begins

Getting students to show up. That's where it all begins.

We can't always assume students will be there when the doors open. Some have no interest in coming through those doors. Sadly, some students don't even know the doors exist. In the last few decades, it's become harder and harder to get non-Christian kids to simply walk through the front doors of our ministries.

When I graduated from college, I volunteered for a church with the same dozen kids who showed up to our little program every Sunday. A church down the street had 200 students each week. Another church around the corner had just three students show up regularly. Why? And more importantly, what about the 1,485 teenagers on the campus down the street—the ones who weren't going to any church? Who was reaching out to them?

At that time I started wondering how we could reach those students. I'd quickly dream up events and programs for that purpose, but every time I gave the idea any further consideration, I was overwhelmed with questions:

- How do we invite unchurched kids to church?

- Why would they want to go to church?

- What are we doing that's worth inviting non-Christian kids to attend?

- Do we need to invite them or *go* to them?

- Is on-campus ministry the answer?

- Can we even do on-campus ministry?

- Is a big outreach event the answer?

- What kinds of events would really draw unchurched kids?

- How can we pull off an event like this?

- Should we start a weekly outreach program?

- What kinds of outreach programs work?

- How do we plan outreach events?

- How do we get non-Christian kids to even show up at these things?

I soon discovered there isn't just one answer to all of these questions, unfortunately.

But that was my problem—I was looking for "the" answer. Instead of finding my own answers, I was trying to find a quick fix for a huge need. That's like trying to find one accounting principle for eliminating the national debt. It isn't that simple.

That's when I met my friend, Jim.

Jim networked with youth workers from around the city. He introduced me to guys who ran teen centers that reached students who were looking for a place to just hang out. He introduced me to a family that ran a sports ministry reaching students on campus after school. He introduced me to churches that ran different outreaches reaching different types of teenagers. I must have met 50 different people running 50 different types of ministries reaching 50 different kinds of kids.

Which one was "the" answer?

None of them.

All of them.

And that's when Jim said to me: *Diverse ministries reach diverse groups of kids.* No one had "the" answer. But all of these ministries had answers. And slowly, my questions were being answered.

I discovered that if I put in the groundwork, some students would show up at church. Some students would show up at events. Some would show up at weekly campus programs. Some preferred off-campus programs. Some would show up in homes, some in garages, and some in teen centers. Some only responded to elaborate programs, and some didn't care, just as long as it was a place to hang out.

IT'S NOT JUST ABOUT SHOWING UP

Getting students to show up was only the beginning. Many of these ministries not only shared Christ with students, but they also plugged them into the local church body, discipled them, and equipped them to reach out to others.

where it all begins

After we get teenagers in the door and reach out to them with the truth, then we can apply what we've learned in all of the other youth ministry books we've read: Discipleship; student leadership; worship; prayer; planning the purpose for our youth group; small groups; mission trips; those diagrams shaped like pyramids, pies, and targets with numerous key components of ministry; and the three-column charts representing three different elements of ministry (e.g., evangelism, discipleship, and service). These are all great tools to help us help teenagers grow in their faith.

I've seen some incredible ministries with a simple, two-fold approach: **Outreach** and **spiritual growth**. Everything these ministries did was about one or the other. They not only ran outreach activities and events and won people to Christ, but they also provided opportunities for students to grow in their faith through one-on-one discipleship, weekly programs, and in-home fellowship groups. Students at these churches were being reached for Christ *and* growing in their faith.

But none of these good things will necessarily get students to walk in the door. So we're back to square one: *How do we get them there in the first place?*

It all starts with groundwork that helps us initiate first contact. That's what this book is all about.

LEARNING FROM OUR MISTAKES

A wise person once said, "Learning from our mistakes is a good thing." But a wiser person added, "Learning from someone else's mistakes is even better."

Many of the chapters in this book provide you with an opportunity to learn from the countless programming mistakes that I and other youth workers have made over the years. You may feel a little of our pain just reading about them, but hopefully you'll do more than that. My desire is that you'll learn to *steer clear* of these blunders and avoid experiencing the same consequences firsthand.

No worries—I won't just abandon you to hash out these poignant yet catastrophic tales. I've also provided some helpful planning methods, along with examples of programming successes. You'll get a glimpse of outreach programming that *gets students to show up.*

I pray these failures and successes—along with a few tidbits of knowledge I've learned along the way—may be of some assistance as you plan future outreach programs, activities, and events that will make an impact for the kingdom. Enjoy!

—*Jonathan*

the field of dreams myth
if you build it, they will come...right?

Many of us remember *Field of Dreams*, the 1989 Kevin Costner film about an Iowa farmer who hears a voice telling him to build a baseball diamond in the middle of his cornfield: *If you build it, he will come.*

Nice movie, bad event-planning philosophy.

During the past decade that I've been a speaker, I've attended literally hundreds of youth ministry events where individuals used the *Field of Dreams* event-planning method. They "feel led" to put on a youth event, and they do so "in faith."

"How many do you expect?" I always ask.

"Thousands," they respond. "We've invited the whole town."

Sounds great.

But fewer than 10 percent of the expected attendees show up.

The intentions were good. And faith can move mountains. So what happened?

What about the suburban youth pastor who plans a youth rally and tells all his students to "bring their friends"? More than 1,000 flyers are passed out at three different high schools. Posters are hung at every school. Hundreds of teenagers are expected. Fewer than 60 show up.

Why?

What went wrong?

Or did anything go wrong? Is "fewer than 60" okay?

A little church in Texas launches a weekly youth program. The youth worker labels it an "outreach program." The church is in a small town, so they'd be happy having 20 students a week. But on the first Wednesday, only seven show up. The next week—five. The following week, the same five show up again.

"Numbers aren't important anyway," the youth worker reasons. "If we can make a difference in just one kid's life, that would be okay."

But what if, realistically, there are at least 100 other students in the neighborhood who haven't even been asked? Is one kid still okay?

It's September and every school in a certain California district has launched its school clubs. A 16-year-old sophomore girl who really knows her Bible wants to reach her high school campus through a lunchtime Bible club. So she tells her church friends about it and organizes the first meeting. Three of her friends show up, along with a freshman from another church. The girls smile and greet the freshman cordially. They talk amongst themselves for a while and then plan their first activity.

the field of dreams myth

The same five students show up at the next meeting, which lasts only 14 minutes (after all, lunch period is really short); the next meeting is canceled because the leader has an orthodontist appointment; and the final meeting draws three of the original girls (they assume the freshman couldn't make it).

"This campus just isn't interested in Jesus," the leader concludes. "There's nothing we can do but shake the dust off our feet."

What happened?

Can't Bible clubs reach a campus? What about that Bible club we heard about across town—the one that had a ton of students?

Do any of these situations sound familiar? Shouldn't the efforts of those who just attempt to build a program be rewarded? Aren't faith and intentions good enough? If we build it, why *won't* they come?

Field of Dreams was a good movie, but this isn't a dream. It's time to wake up!

aligning our defining
"outreach" that actually reaches out

The word *outreach* is slapped onto the titles of a variety of programs. It's a buzzword that's probably thrown around a lot more than it's actually thought about.

I've been to hundreds of "outreach" programs where no reaching out took place. Instead, the purpose of these programs always seemed to be worship or helping Christians grow in their faith. Noble purposes, indeed—but not "outreach" by any means.

I've spoken at "outreach" rallies where the first thing out of the emcee's mouth is "How many of you are here to celebrate Jesus?"

Think about that for a second.

How many students who aren't believers do you think came to that event to "celebrate Jesus"? Granted, many of these "rallies" are full of Christians who scream in excitement and yell in celebration, so the statement isn't usually received poorly. But what's wrong with this picture?

I see two oversights:

1. *Why is our audience 90 percent Christians?* We're talking about an **outreach** program, right? At an **outreach** program we might want to draw teenagers who don't believe in Jesus yet. Do you remember Jeff Goldblum's character in *Jurassic Park*? During that first uneventful tour of the park, he says, "Now eventually you might have dinosaurs on your dinosaur tour, right?" He taps on the camera. "Hello? Yes?"

So why aren't the "outreach kids" attending? Didn't our church kids believe us when we said, "Bring your friends who need to hear about Jesus"? The sad truth: **Our audience is often made up of the wrong students**. No wonder they didn't object when we yelled, "How many of you are here to celebrate Jesus?"

Which leads us to our second blunder.

2. *If we're trying to draw out **unbelievers**, then why are we talking to them as though they're* already *Christians?* Imagine you're asked to emcee the *MTV Music Awards*. The arena is decorated. All of the hottest artists have walked the red carpet and taken their seats. The crowd is full of screaming music fans. Now the program begins, and you walk onstage and yell, "How many of you are here to celebrate Jesus?"

Awkward.

None of us would yell such a phrase to that crowd. So why do we do it at our "outreach" events?

The truth of the matter is this: Many of us label our programs "outreach," but we don't always draw the students we're supposed to reach. Even if we do, we often talk to them as if they're Christians. Why?

What if some of the difficulty lies in the fact that we don't really know much about this "animal" we're attempting to tame? We've never taken the time to really look at our goals for this kind of programming and put it into words. We never took the time to define it.

Maybe we should try to identify exactly whom we're targeting and what we're trying to achieve.

DEFINING AN OUTREACH PROGRAM

The following is a sample definition we can use as a tool to keep us accountable to our goal of reaching out. This isn't THE definition; it's simply one way to define whom we're targeting and what we're trying to achieve.

> OUTREACH PROGRAM: *An event, activity, or program used as a means to attract those who don't know Jesus and* point them to Jesus.

Breaking It Down
I'd like to make three key observations about the above definition.

1. You'll need to decide how you're going to "point them to Jesus." That's the goal of everything we're doing here. If "pointing them to Jesus" is our purpose, how are we going to do it?

I know it seems basic, but you'd be surprised by the number of youth events I attend every year where no one knows the purpose of the event. The whole reason most of us do outreach events is so we can point people toward Jesus. I don't know about you, but I'm really not in the business of feeding teenagers pizza or selling tickets to a basketball tournament. I want to impact students' lives with the life-changing message of Jesus Christ. So first things first: Figure out how we're going to **point them to Jesus**.

The most common way is to share the gospel message. If this is your specific purpose, then everything you do during the program should point toward sharing the gospel. Don't let anything interfere with it. Don't let your "cool game" run so long that the speaker has less time to share God's truth or the counselors don't have time to meet with students one-on-one.

Sharing the gospel isn't the only way to **point them to Jesus**. Chapter 3 will show us several different examples of how to do it, and it will also guide us through the process of selecting our **purpose** and keeping our eyes fixed on that goal.

But *purpose* isn't the only important part of this definition.

2. You need a draw to "attract those who don't know Jesus."
We can't achieve our purpose if no one is there. What will get them there? Our definition says we need to "attract those who don't know Jesus." How are we going to do that? What will attract them?

One of the most neglected elements I see in programs across the country is **draw**. Most people just book a band and a speaker. Sound familiar?

Forget about our church kids for a second. Have we ever stopped to ask a teenager who's never been to church if he's even remotely interested in coming out to listen to some Christian band and Jonathan McKee? His answer would probably be, "Who and who?"

So what works? Don't worry. In chapter 4 we'll not only reinforce the necessity of **draw**, but we'll also give several examples that work.

But the definition doesn't end with **purpose** and **draw**. It also talks about our **target audience**. Hence, my third observation about our definition of *outreach program* follows.

3. REMEMBER: YOUR AUDIENCE IS "THOSE WHO DON'T KNOW JESUS." SO DON'T TREAT THEM LIKE THEY DO! One of the worst things we can do to non-Christians is make them feel like they don't belong. Yet we do it all the time.

I won't spend a lot of time on this point. I devoted an entire book to the subject of understanding and reaching unchurched teenagers called *Do They Run When They See You Coming? Reaching Out to Unchurched Teenagers* (Youth Specialties/Zondervan, 2005). But if our audience is filled with "those who don't know Jesus," we shouldn't talk to them as if they've grown up in the church. They didn't come to worship God. Why do we assume they did? They're probably there because some cute sophomore invited them, or they heard free pizza was being served.

So don't talk to them in a language they don't understand. They don't know what "salvation" is. They don't know what a "testimony" is or even what the word *Christian* means. After all, 81 percent of Americans claim to be "Christian." But where are they every Sunday? Do you think they know what that word really means?

Don't talk about "non-believers" or "the lost." Prep the speakers, the emcee, and the band not to talk about how we "need to be a light to non-Christians." *"Psssst! Stop talking about them! They're sitting right there!"*

And as we mentioned earlier in the chapter, don't turn it into a pep rally for believers. Don't start the event with an emcee onstage hyping up the audience with, "HOW MANY

BELIEVERS WE GOT IN DA HEY-OUSE?!" If there *is* a non-Christian there (and hopefully there's at least one present, since this is an *outreach* event), how is she supposed to respond? Why not just yell, "Hello, Cincinnati!" Or, if you want to pump it up like a pep rally, break it down by grade. "How many freshmen we got in the house?"

The key to reaching our audience is *knowing* our audience. And the 411 on any outreach audience is this: They don't know Jesus. So don't treat them as though they do.

Define It

Now we have a working definition for an outreach program that identifies precisely whom we're targeting and exactly what we're trying to achieve.

> OUTREACH PROGRAM: An event, activity, or program used as a means to attract those who don't know Jesus and point them to Jesus.

Remember:

> 1. You'll need to decide **how** you're going to **point them to Jesus**.

> 2. You need a **draw** to **attract** those who don't know Jesus.

> 3. Remember your **audience**—"**those who don't know Jesus**." Don't treat them like they do!

doing it "on purpose"
pointing where we want to point

Why are you doing this event?

> "To give fathers and sons something to do together."

> "To offer Christians some good clean entertainment."

> "To bring out people who don't know Jesus and share the gospel with them."

> "To challenge our leaders to share their faith."

These purposes for doing an event all seem noble, but very different.

So what's the problem?

All of these responses were from *different* people describing the *same* two-hour event. They just didn't know **why** they were doing the event.

That's why I often ask youth leaders questions such as, "Why did you put on your last event?" or "What was the purpose of your last program?"

The first question I ask youth leaders when they ask me to speak is, "What is the purpose of this event?" If a youth leader wants me to speak during her weekly Wednesday night program, the first question I ask is, "Why do you do this Wednesday night program?"

And often the answer is, "Because we've always had a Wednesday night program!" How many times have you heard this response?

Sorry. "Because we've always done it that way" is not the purpose of a program.

Before we embark on any event planning, we should always know our destination. In this book we're specifically talking about planning *outreach* programs. So for our purposes, let's return to our definition of the outreach program:

> OUTREACH PROGRAM: *An event, activity, or program used as a means to attract those who don't know Jesus and* point them to Jesus.

As we discussed in chapter 2, our purpose for any outreach program will be to **point them to Jesus**. This isn't debatable. By our own definition, the reason we're planning a program at all is so we can point people to Jesus.

That's our focus. Everything we do needs to aim for that goal. We need to be careful not to let any of our methodology interfere with this purpose. In other words, don't let the activities drag on so long that we don't have time to point them to Jesus, the very thing we set out to do!

I'll never forget the group that planned a huge event with a carnival of fun activities, and a dynamic program with music, drama, and a speaker. Their programming was so involved, in fact, that they simply ran out of time. They were actually 10 minutes away from introducing the speaker when the facility started closing down and everyone had to leave.

They forgot their purpose.

Our goal is to **point them to Jesus**. Don't let anything else get in the way of that.

But does pointing them to Jesus mean you have to have someone stand up and share the gospel at every event? Is that the only way to do an outreach program? Is that all that Jesus modeled? After every miracle did he whip out an easel and draw two cliffs and a cross bridging the gap?

The fact is we can point people to Jesus in numerous ways. I've narrowed them down to three broad categories.

A. SHARE THE GOSPEL

This is a no-brainer. Create opportunities to share Christ with students once we get them out to our programs, activities, or events. We can do this with a speaker, movie, drama, or even music. I share the gospel at almost 80 percent of my outreach events or programs.

However, we shouldn't plan on just sharing the message, shutting out the lights, and leaving. We need to give them an opportunity to respond. We should have a plan for talking with the people individually and creating a means for follow up. I usually have them raise a hand or come forward to meet with a counselor who can talk with them about the decision they made. I also use decision cards. If students meet with counselors, I have counselors fill out the cards for them— legibility is very important—noting their contact information, what decision they made (first-time decision, rededication, and so on), and what group, if any, they came with. These cards are vital and provide the groundwork for follow up.

Billy Graham's organization has been doing a fantastic job with this for decades. Billy doesn't just come to a city, preach, and leave. His organization comes a year in advance, training counselors, meeting with hundreds of area churches, and implementing a plan for following up with all the new believers. What an incredible example of faith and diligence. It's a year before the invitation is even given; yet they're planning for thousands to come forward. Faith and elbow grease working hand in hand.

On the night of a Billy Graham Crusade, those who come forward meet with counselors and hear the gospel one-on-one. Then they have an opportunity to make a decision. Everyone who comes forward then fills out a follow-up card. This is a great way to clarify the commitment they've made, and it sets the stage for following up with the person effectively.

Billy Graham's organization shares the gospel responsibly. Don't be afraid to mimic their methodology. We'll look at more examples of how to (and how not to) share the gospel and give an invitation later in this book.

B. DEMONSTRATE GOD'S LOVE WITH AN ACT OF SERVICE

Do you *have* to share the gospel to point to Jesus? Or consider this question: Was Mother Theresa a great evangelist?

Our actions often point to Jesus more effectively than our words do. The most famous "evangelism" passages in the Bible seem to talk more about actions than words. Think about it: God wants us to be salt and light in our world—"In the same way, let your light shine before men, that they may *see your good deeds* and praise your Father in heaven" (Matthew 5:16, emphasis mine).

getting students to show up

Or how about 1 Peter 3:15—"Always be prepared to give an answer to everyone who asks you to give *the reason for the hope that you have*" (emphasis mine). Some people like to emphasize the part of this verse that says, "Always be prepared." So we memorize four laws and go looking for people to share them with. Except—that's not what the verse says. Look carefully. According to the verse, we need to have "the hope" in our lives. People need to notice something different about us. When the world is crumbling, they'll see "the hope" in our lives. And just maybe they'll ask us, "Hey, everything stinks right now, but you still seem to have hope. Why? What's the reason for this hope?"

Now read the verse one more time: "Always be prepared to give an answer to everyone who asks you to give *the reason for the hope that you have.*"

We can have "the hope." We can show "good deeds" and point people to Jesus.

Believe it or not, **demonstrating God's love** can be the purpose of an event—the type of event where people see Jesus through the example of his followers. The gospel doesn't have to be shared because Christ is exemplified through the actions of his people. Your words are only half as important as your actions. No matter what "draw" you choose, make sure everyone involved knows the purpose of this event is serving selflessly so others can see God in your actions.

A few years back, our ministry had a contest where youth ministers from around the world submitted ideas for "out of the box" outreach—creative outreach ideas they'd successfully used with their own groups. I'll never forget one idea that a youth pastor named Marty from Centerville, Ohio submitted:

> Have your congregation donate new nine-volt batteries to your youth group for a few weeks. Then hand them out (or install them yourselves),

in Jesus' name, in the church's neighborhood. The batteries are for their smoke detectors...take along a clipboard, paper, and a pen to take down the neighbor's prayer requests...plenty of ministry to be had by all! The reason this worked was because we didn't do the expected—try to convert people. We just met a need (batteries in smoke detectors) and offered to pray for them. The neighbors were shocked (no pun intended). They really couldn't believe it. The youth were really charged (I did it again...) to show *God's* love so practically!

I love Marty's example. They didn't set up easels in living rooms or drop off gospel tracts. They just met a need. Meeting needs and offering to pray for people created opportunities for conversation. And yes, 1 Peter 3:15 notes that we need to be ready for these opportunities. Just don't force them. If people notice the "hope" in us and *ask* us about it, then we need to be ready to answer them. But it all starts by just **demonstrating his love**.

Other examples of events or programs where we demonstrate his love might be service projects, feeding the homeless, or even providing free goods or services in his name.

C. INVITE THEM TO CHURCH OR YOUTH GROUP

Another way we can point people toward Jesus is by inviting them to hear more about Jesus. Yet, we don't actually have to share everything the first time we meet someone. We can just invite them to come back.

If there's one thing I've learned about evangelism in the new millennium—it's much more about conversations than presentations. And good conversations take time.

Our events can simply have the purpose of **inviting them back**. Why do we feel as though we have to do it all in one night? The whole goal of an event could be to just show them a fun time and invite them back.

The church around the corner recently hosted a junior high event called "Pizza Feed." Their youth group of about 30 students put on an event in the church gym, and every kid was encouraged to bring friends. The leaders and the students worked hard, and almost 100 teenagers showed up. They ate pizza, beat each other up in an inflatable boxing ring, laughed, hung out, and just had a good time. Ten minutes before the event was scheduled to end, they pulled everyone together, and then the staff did a funny skit, they announced their upcoming activities and trips, and a student from the youth group briefly shared about his life. He talked about some problems he'd experienced the previous year and how through this youth group he'd found people to talk to and answers to some of life's questions. During this part of the event, Jesus was mentioned, but no invitation was given. Then the youth leader handed out flyers inviting everyone back for the next week.

What was the purpose of this event? Was it outreach?

Yes. Remember our definition of *outreach program*? This youth group invited teenagers who **didn't know Jesus** with the **draw** of pizza. Then they **pointed them to Jesus** by giving them a glimpse of a place where they could go and find out more about him. The purpose of the event was to reach out to students who don't go to church and simply invite them to church.

Not bad, huh?

Other inviting events could be carnivals, car shows, picnics, or even acts of community service where an "invite" to church is given.

doing it "on purpose"

THE NEED FOR PURPOSE

Don't get caught planning an event without first knowing your goal or purpose. If you want to plan an outreach event, you must first decide what your goal will be. Do you want to share the gospel? Do you want to show Christ's love with an act of service? Or maybe you just want to invite people to church. Regardless of which one you choose, in the planning of *any* event, you need to determine your **purpose**.

Even so, the purpose won't necessarily get students to come to the event. So how can we **draw** them in?

I'm so glad you asked.

Let's talk about that in the next chapter...

jell-o wrestling, root beer kegs, and slam dunks

the importance of "draw"

A few years ago, I exited the freeway in my rental car and drove toward the small East Coast town where I was scheduled to speak that evening. As I navigated my way through the center of town, I drove under a huge banner strung between two streetlights:

FRIDAY NIGHT YOUTH RALLY

SPEAKER: JONATHAN MCKEE

I pulled into the parking lot of the local high school. Ten minutes later I was talking with the youth worker who booked me to speak at the youth rally that night.

"Did you see the sign?" he asked.

"Yeah…hard to miss that one."

"The fire department hung it up for us."

We talked a little about the event. I wasn't involved in the planning; I was just booked as a speaker. But I was curious to know how he was going to draw students to the rally, so I asked him, "What's your draw?"

He looked at me for a second and then pointed to me with a smile. "Well, *you* are. That's why we booked you."

Uh oh!

I didn't have to ask him any more questions. I now had a good idea what the attendance would look like for the evening.

Let me be clear about something: Jonathan McKee is NOT a draw. I'm the guy who's going to grab the crowd's attention once they show up, and I'm the guy who's going to share the gospel in a relevant way, but I'm not a draw.

Let me take this a step further: Think of the best Christian youth speakers you've ever heard. Okay, do you have these people in your mind? Good. Now read this next sentence very closely: **They are *not* a draw!** Non-Christian teenagers don't have a desire to hear a speaker, period. They will *listen* to a speaker once they're in the room. But that's not what draws them to the event in the first place.

Imagine a teenager trying to make a decision about what to do on a Friday night:

Go to the movies...or hear a speaker.

Hang out with my friends...or hear a speaker.

Go to my girlfriend's house when her parents are away...or hear a speaker.

Youth ministry just can't compete. Something else has to "draw" students there.

NO DRAW...NO STUDENTS

I've been involved in several programs where the planning organizations invite a speaker to do public school assemblies during the week, followed by a big outreach rally at the end of the week. Everyone seems to run the show the exact same way. *Get the speaker into as many schools as possible, and then have the speaker invite all the students to come to the rally.* The results are always the same. A very small percentage of students actually show up.

Why?

Maybe the speaker was bad—right?

Not in the programs I saw. I saw some fantastic speakers who used humor or compelling testimonials. Teenagers were on the edge of their seats. And at the end of these assemblies, students actually seemed eager to attend the end-of-the-week rally. But somehow, they just don't make it there. The rally might have been well attended by partnering churches, but not by the students from the school assemblies.

Again, what's the draw? When it actually comes to Friday night, regardless of how good the speaker was, will students really skip out on all of their other options so they can go hear a speaker? Maybe some teenagers will—especially the ones who have no other social options. That's why rallies like these can often draw crowds of younger teens. They have nothing else to do.

But even with younger kids it can be difficult to get students to attend because of another factor: *The gatekeeper.* That's right. I'm referring to the teenagers' parents who then have to decide whether or not *they* want little Johnny to go hear the speaker. And if little Johnny needs a ride from his parents, then the chances are even slimmer that he'll attend.

So what do you do?

Understand the importance of "draw."

Let's go back to the truths derived from our definition introduced in chapter 2.

> OUTREACH PROGRAM: An event, activity, or program used as a means to attract those who don't know Jesus and point them to Jesus.

You need a **draw** to **attract** those who don't know Jesus. Something other than a speaker needs to get them there. Sure, a good speaker helps, but a speaker is rarely the primary draw for teenagers.

WHAT WORKS?

So what does "draw" students out on a Friday night?

Let's start with a no-brainer. FREE FOOD.

That's right. Free pizza will draw hundreds more teenagers than Jonathan McKee ever will. Teenagers like food! And pizza is a youth outreach event staple.

Consider the above example of a group doing public school assemblies. Add free pizza to the equation on a Friday night, and you've just increased your percentages.

Why stop there?

How about adding some door prizes to the equation? Do you know anyone who owns a small retail business? Can you get store owners to donate a bike, an iPod, a CD player, or some gift certificates? Or what if you just include some of these items in your event's budget?

Now back to those school assemblies. The speaker announces he'll be speaking at a rally on Friday night and there will be free pizza and great door prizes. Maybe he even names a few of the giveaways: "We'll be giving away a CD player!" A $29 dollar portable CD player from Wal-Mart will increase your attendance percentages even more.

Why stop there?

What about using sporting events as a draw? Slam-dunk contests, skateboarding, beach volleyball—whatever is a popular teenage activity in your area. One element about draws we need to understand is that **draws vary from place to place.** A two-on-two basketball tournament might be hot in one town, while a soccer match might be a bigger draw in another. We need to learn to observe what teenagers are doing, where they go for fun, and how they spend their money. These observations will clue us in to effective draws for our events.

Sporting events can be very successful draws—either as the main element of the event or as an extra. Our entire event might be "Skatefest," a huge skateboarding event. Or we might just include a skateboarding exhibition to our Friday night assembly plan. (Yep, you guessed it. We just increased our percentages even more!)

What about bands or music? Can they be a draw?

Music is a double-edged sword. Thirty years ago youth ministries could hire a "rock band" and draw a ton of teenagers. The problem now is that today's music is pretty diverse. And I'm not talking about rock, rap, country, and so on. Music has divided itself into even more specific subcategories with

jell-o wrestling, root beer kegs, and slam dunks

five different kinds of rock, different types of hip-hop—each bringing out specific crowds.

Where music used to be a general draw, now it serves more as a target-market draw. We can't just say, "A band will be there!" Most teenagers want to know, "Who?" or "What kind of band?"

Don't get me wrong. Music can be a huge draw. **We just need to realize whom we're targeting**. And that leads me to another point that I'm almost afraid to mention. (It might seem as though I'm meddling with some people's religion when I bring up this next point.) But I'll write it anyway: *To effectively draw the students in our communities with music, we need to provide the style of music they want to hear, not the style we want to hear.*

Back in 2005, a Kaiser Family Foundation survey found that among 7th through 12th graders who listened to music in a typical day, 65 percent favored rap/hip-hop; coming in second was alternative rock, attracting 32 percent of listeners. *So... why were the overwhelming majority of youth workers booking rock bands for events where I spoke in 2005?*

My point is simple: **Know your audience**. Take a look around and notice what kinds of music teenagers are listening to in your area and give them that music. When I was running a campus ministry at a junior high school, I quickly realized every kid in the school listened to the same local hip-hop radio station. So once a year I booked a local Christian rapper to do a concert. It was one of the biggest draws of the year.

In contrast, I know a church across town that sits in an area with many rock music fans. So they have a "concert café" that brings out about 400 students every Friday night to hear a rock band. Different genre, same goal. **Know your audience**.

Target marketing? Yes.

Effective? Yes.

Creative Speakers—the "Anti-Repellent"

You've already heard me get up on my soapbox about how speakers are *not* a draw. But many events and programs include a speaker. How can we let students know there will be a speaker at our event without deterring our draw in the process?

It's a good idea to let people know in advance that you're going to have a speaker. I like to be very upfront with students. That way they won't feel blindsided when they get to an event: *Hey, I didn't know they were going to preach to me!*

So how do we let them know what's on the program agenda without losing them?

Good question.

The answer is the "anti-repellent" speaker.

That's right. We already know our speaker is most likely not a draw for students. So the only thing we need to do is book a speaker who's not a repellent.

How do we do that?

The key is to book a speaker with some creative quality like humor, a powerful story, celebrity status, or a certain skill or talent. Your flyer should never just read Speaker—Jonathan McKee. It should always read something like Hilarious Speaker— Matt Furby. Or Speaker—BMX Stunt Rider, Tony Alvarez. Or Speaker—Hip-Hop Sensation, Fred Lynch.

Yes, the speaker may not be a draw, but don't allow the speaker to be a repellent, either.

The Relational Draw

Teenagers want to go to "the place to be." They want to go where "everyone" is hanging out. Whenever I visit campus and talk with students about upcoming events, the first question out of their mouths is, "Who's going to be there?"

One year while I was running a campus ministry with struggling attendance numbers, I met a kid on campus who was the best player on the basketball team. I started hanging out and playing basketball with him at lunchtime. Before long, he and his friends started coming to our program. And then something amazing happened—the group's attendance exploded. Somehow the presence of just one teenager put an invisible stamp of approval on our program, which brought out more students, and eventually it was the "place to be" on Wednesday nights.

More Draws

There are endless ideas for draws. The draw can be the program itself, such as attractive theme nights like "*Kung Fu* Film Night" or "*Fear Factor* Night" or an "*American Idol* Talent Show." Or off-the-wall ideas of things teenagers can't normally do but want to do. Every year a youth group in Kansas hosts a Winter Beach Party. They rent an indoor pool at the local college, bring in sand and fake palm trees, serve little drinks with umbrellas in them, and have a fantastic swimming party! The novelty of this event is the draw. (We provide endless examples of these kinds of events on our ministry's free Web site: www.TheSourceForYouthMinistry.com. Just click on "Event Ideas.")

The bottom line is this: If we don't draw students out, then we can't achieve our purpose. In other words, if we want to reach 'em, we need to get 'em there!

Start by getting to know your area. Learn what teenagers like to do and align your draw with their interests. Then watch 'em come out.

But how do you start?

Good question. Let's look at the entire planning process in the next chapter.

staring at a blank piece of paper
the planning process—starting from scratch

It's already on the calendar. The event will be called "LOL" or *Laugh Out Loud* in "texting" or instant messenger abbreviations, a common language used by today's generation of teenagers. One of your interns came up with the idea a long time ago, and your teenagers thought it sounded great.

But you only know two elements so far: *Your purpose and your draw.* You've prayed about the event and you feel God's leading. The purpose will be to share the gospel. The draw: Free pizza, three crazy videos, and a funny speaker (who alone isn't a draw, but the fact that he's a comedian adds to this event because it means he probably won't be *boring*). In addition, the event itself is a big draw because you're in a small town, and there's *nothing* else for teenagers to do on a Friday night.

So now what?

You stare at a blank piece of paper on your desk. You write the word PURPOSE across the top. Next to it, you write TO SHARE THE GOSPEL.

Under that you write the word DRAW. Next to it you write PIZZA, VIDEOS, DOOR PRIZES, CRAZY VIDEOS, FUNNY SPEAKER—AND EVERYONE'S GOING TO BE THERE!

Now you're cooking!

But what do you do next?

No worries. The worst is actually over. The draw is the most difficult element to discover. And not all purposes and draws work well together. So if you have your purpose and draw nailed, you're halfway there!

THE PROCESS

Let's look at the entire planning process for organizing programs, activities, or events. I'll use LOL, the big citywide event I mentioned above, as an example throughout this chapter to help you understand the process.

We don't need to spend too much time talking about your *purpose* and *draw*, since we've already spent a chapter talking about each of these elements. But to be thorough and to make our process complete, I'll quickly include

Note: Don't let the following numbers scare you. *Some of them might seem large for individual ministries, but don't worry—these numbers are large for most of us. Remember—they represent a big event. However, this process still works for weekly programs, one-time events, church programs, on-campus programs, big programs, or even small programs. I'm just using the example of a large citywide event (and I'll go into much more detail about this in chapter 9) because with large events, these steps are more pronounced. You have more time to do the steps and more resources to accomplish them. But these are the same steps I used years ago when planning an outreach event for 25 teenagers. And these are the same steps we're going to use in the next few chapters as we consider planning a small weekly outreach ministry and a campus outreach program.*

staring at a blank piece of paper

them in the programming process and talk about the specifics of this event.

1. Pray

When planning any event, the best place to start is on your knees. Pray and ask God what he wants you to do. Don't wait until the night of the event to ask "for the Spirit's leading." Talk to him about it now. The Spirit will lead you during the planning. It's not like God is going to show up on the night of the event, look around the audience for the first time, and say, "I didn't know those students were going to be here. We need to change everything!" God knows who's going to be there. Bring him into the process from the very beginning and keep him in the process until the very end.

2. Plan Your Purpose

Not only is this the most important element of the program, but it's also the *first* element you should plan. Know the goal of your program before you begin brainstorming your draw or what the program might look like. In the example of LOL, your purpose will be to share the gospel with those who don't know Jesus. This demands a really great draw because you need to get a lot of unchurched teenagers there!

3. Pinpoint Your Target Audience

Who are you trying to draw?

Don't skip this question—it will help you in several areas. First, it may keep you to your purpose. With LOL, we said the purpose was *to share the gospel with those who don't know Jesus*. So that narrows down the target audience to unbelievers. But you need to be even more specific. What age range are you trying to bring out to this event? From what areas? Are you targeting a specific type of kid, a specific school, or a specific gender?

You may choose to target junior and senior high students from your region, specifically those who don't know Jesus. And depending on your location, you may define "region" as anywhere within an hour of your location.

Other events might have a draw that's even narrower. You might want to draw out just the "skaters" or teenagers who like a specific genre of music. Focusing on such specific "target markets" is completely acceptable; you just need to know who that market is so you can focus your draw on that particular audience.

4. Brainstorm Your Draw

Brainstorm the best possible draw that would bring teenagers out to achieve your purpose. During the brainstorming process, no idea is bad. Dream up even the most crazy, impossible things. Discover what teenagers like to do—and run with it. (I won't reiterate the basics here, since chapter 4 covered this step in detail.)

LOL has several draws. The first is its name. What event would you rather go to—one called "LOL" or "Town Youth Rally"? A catchy name can really help an event. Most teenagers probably haven't heard of an event called "LOL" before, so this will be something new. And "new" is always better than "the same old thing."

A second draw is the free pizza. As I already mentioned in chapter 4, teenagers like food and you can't beat the price of FREE. But keep in mind that offering something for free means you're going to have some serious budgeting issues later on in the process. You have to find the funds to pay for that "free food" somehow. It's not impossible; I've done it numerous times with the help of generous donors. But if it's too difficult for your budget, then you might just charge a couple of bucks and change your Free Pizza to a $5 cover charge that includes All-You-Can-Eat Pizza!

The funny videos are a third draw. When you brainstormed about the event, someone came up with the idea that youth groups could submit videos for the "LOL Funniest Video Contest." As you kicked the idea around the room, you decided not to limit it to just youth groups—after all, this is to be an outreach event. So you set up the guidelines, due dates, and time limitations, and spread the word about the contest to all the local schools. Then you made sure at least a couple of youth groups were committed to making videos so you wouldn't end up empty handed on the night of the event.

In addition to draw potential, a video contest is also a good way to get people involved in future events. Students love to watch themselves and their friends on tape. Just realize that this is one of those elements of an event that might be hard to deliver the first year, but a momentum will build for following years. Students will see the videos and say, "I could have done one of those. Next year, let's do one!"

The fourth and final draw for the LOL event will be the door prizes. Advertise that you'll be giving away an MP3 player, gift certificates, skateboards, and basketball tickets. Did you notice the variety of prizes that will attract different groups of students? Yes, you'll have to pound the pavement in order to get these prizes donated. You may even have to purchase some of them. But you'll be amazed how many donations you'll receive when you send out a letter asking local merchants to donate something to your "nonprofit event." (See the appendix for a sample donor letter.) And I bet you'll be surprised when you discover how many of these resources are sitting beside you in church on Sunday morning.

The draw is what attracts people to the event. You can't overdo your draw.

5. Consider Your Resources

Now it's time to get back to reality. You've just brainstormed a lot of fun ideas that add up to a whole lot of money. So you ask your church treasurer how much money is in the existing youth ministry budget.

"Exactly $43.79."

Hmmmm. I guess you may need to rethink a couple things. You need to take all of your good brainstorming ideas and incorporate them with your existing resources. In other words, you need to ask yourself a few questions: *What resources do we have? What resources can we acquire? Can we really pull this thing off?*

ONE RESOURCE TO CONSIDER IS YOUR ROUGH BUDGET. Go through the event in your mind and make a list of anything that could cost you money. Think of the set-up. Do you have to rent any trucks or trailers? Do you have to feed your workers? Do you have to rent your facility? Do you have to rent chairs, staging, or lights? Are there any props or prizes you have to buy? What about signs, posters, flyers, or mailers?

Just keep asking yourself how much each item costs. If you want to serve pizza, ask yourself how much it will cost. Will you put it on plates? Will you serve drinks? Will these drinks require cups? Do you need napkins? Do you have tables to serve the pizza on? What if there's a spill—do you already have a mop? Do you need security guards armed with automatic weapons?

I list all of these items in my preliminary budget. It doesn't have to be anything fancy, just a list of the items and how much each one costs. Here's what your list might look like, based on the above brainstorming:

staring at a blank piece of paper

LOL EVENT BUDGET:

Facility: FREE (our church)

Lighting: $300 (spotlight and stage light rental)

Sound: FREE (our church)

Workers' Food: $50 (drinks and snacks—they'll eat pizza with the students)

Tables: FREE (our church)

Pizza: $7 for each large (one large pizza feeds three and a half students)

Drinks: $12 for punch mix to serve 100 students

Cups: $7 for 250 cups

Plates: $8 for 300 plates

Napkins: $7 for 500 paper napkins

Videos: FREE

Video Projector: FREE (our church)

Door Prizes: $50 (most prizes will be donated)

Speaker:	$1,000 (national speaker) *Note: I'll talk some more about how to save money when booking a speaker. Just bear with me for a few moments.*
Speaker Travel:	$600 (plane ticket, hotel, food, etc.)
Flyers:	FREE (our church)
Posters:	$137 to get them printed
Mailers:	FREE (our church)
Security Badges:	$45 (for 20 lanyards with plastic badge holders)

Some of the latter costs will vary depending on the attendance figures.

THE ONLY WAY TO FIGURE OUT A PROJECTED ATTENDANCE IS TO MAKE AN EDUCATED GUESS AS TO HOW MANY TEENAGERS YOU'LL HAVE. How do you do that? This is one of those tricky areas when it comes to programming large events. If you've never done this kind of event before, then there's no history to refer to. Will 50 come—or will 500 come? The difference between those two numbers is a whole lot more pizza and a whole lot more budget to work with. How can you predict?

Ticket presales are one great way to help get a rough idea. But don't lose sight of your goal. If your goal is to draw lots of unchurched students to the event, don't ask other churches in the area to buy tickets just for their youth groups. Encourage them to buy tickets for all the unchurched friends that their students will bring. We have to be proactive about communicating this "outreach" mindset from the very beginning.

What if five or six churches owned this event together and each church committed to buying a certain number of tickets and allowing each of their students to invite three friends to attend. Not only would this encourage church kids to invite their friends, but a network of churches would own the event together. As a result, you might get a better idea of expected numbers from your presale results.

Another idea is to offer an "early-bird" rate—$10 FOR ADVANCE TICKETS OR $15 AT THE DOOR. This creates an incentive to buy tickets early, and it also helps you predict final numbers.

All of these methods might help you get a more accurate estimate as to how many students will attend. But sooner or later, you'll have to make an educated guess.

YOU NEED TO GUESS LOW AND YOU NEED TO GUESS HIGH. What? When it comes to guessing how many will attend (i.e., how much *income* you'll bring in), you need to **guess low**. This isn't a lack of faith, it's just plain smart. I've been to numerous events where pastors looked me in the eyes and told me God would bring 750 students out. Unfortunately, they also banked on it. Imagine their disappointment when only 237 teenagers showed up. And what a shame to be disappointed with this kind of attendance. Let me assure you, 237 teenagers showing up to a small-town, first-ever event is *great*! You can do all kinds of things with a budget from 237 teenagers— unless you planned on having 750.

On the other hand, when it comes to your food and supplies, **guess high**. In other words, if you guessed that only 300 will show up, don't buy exactly 300 plates. That won't provide even one plate for your workers. I always buy too many of the cheap items, just in case. Items like pizza, I order about 10 percent more than expected, and I have a back-up plan in case attendance booms. Also use the "eat last" principle—schedule the eating time well into the program so you have time to get more food, if needed. I usually tell the pizza restaurant that I might be ordering some more and arrange it so all we have to do is pick up the phone and tell them "10 more pizzas," and one of my volunteers heads over to pick them up 25 minutes later.

My friend Lane helps organize huge events for a large Christian organization. He likes to set two goals: A "budget-attendance goal" and a "God-sized" goal. The budget-attendance goal is how much you need to receive so you can pay the bills and not get fired. This is what you truly *need*. A God-sized goal is something you ask God to bring. If God brings more—that's great. More teenagers are reached and you have a foundation for the next event. You need to "bank" on your budget-attendance goal, yet have a plan for your God-sized goal.

Once you have your low guess for attendance and high guess for needed supplies, incorporate those numbers into your budget. Let's say, for example's sake, that you "bank" on 300 students for your first year of this LOL event. Here's what the amended budget might look like:

LOL EVENT BUDGET:

Facility:	$0.00
Lighting:	$300.00
Sound:	$0.00
Workers' Food:	$50.00
Tables:	$0.00

Pizza: $714.00 (*$7 for each
                          large pizza; one large
                          pizza feeds three and a
                          half teenagers. 300
                          teenagers divided by
                          3.5 teenagers per
                          pizza = 86 pizzas + 7
                          more pizzas for the
                          workers OR 93 pizzas +
                          9 more for a 10 percent
                          cushion = 102 pizzas.*)

Drinks: $36.00 ($12 for punch
                          mix to serve 100
                          teenagers)

Cups: $14.00 ($7 for 250
                          cups)

Plates: $16.00 ($8 for 300
                          plates)

Napkins: $7.00 (for 500 paper
                          napkins)

Videos: $0.00

Video Projector: $0.00

Door Prizes: $50.00

Speaker: $1,000.00

Speaker Travel: $600.00

Flyers: $0.00

Posters:	$137.00
Mailers:	$0.00
Security Badges:	$45.00
SUBTOTAL:	**$2,969.00**

Think this is all you'll need for the event? Let me share something that's helped me in my event planning. Add 10 percent for a category simply called "Miscellaneous" or "Budget Flexibility." After doing these events for a while, you'll realize this cushion is usually needed when you have to purchase some item you forgot during the planning stages. If not, then you'll just have a bit of a head start for next year's event.

Miscellaneous:	$295.00
TOTAL:	**$3,264.00**

So your total projected cost for the LOL event is $3,264.

How much do you need to collect from each student so you make enough to at least cover your cost of $3,264? Here's where your educated guess about the attendance comes in. You're banking on at least 300 students. Take your total projected cost and divide it by the number of expected students. In this case, take your total cost of $3,264.00 and divide it by 300 students. This equals a cost of $10.88 per student.

The big question you have to ask yourself now is, "Can I charge $10.88 without deterring my draw?" In other words, will teenagers be willing to dish out $11 for a night of comedy, pizza, and potential prizes? I can't answer that question for you—it varies from area to area.

staring at a blank piece of paper

I once volunteered at a church in a very affluent area, and we could charge $20 for any youth event, and it was never a problem. I also worked with a group from a pretty poor area where we lost teenagers any time an event cost over $10.

I've found that a $10 cost is pretty safe these days. Movie tickets cost about that much, and those always seem to be a good comparison point. But we also need to ask ourselves, "In a student's mind, are we providing something of equal value to the ticket price of a movie?"

I don't think the LOL example makes the cut. I'm sure many people would charge $11 a ticket and hope to break even on the event. But personally, I don't think I'd charge that much. I'd be afraid that $11 would be too much for pizza and prizes.

Why do I only mention the pizza and prizes? Because teenagers won't consider a speaker as part of the value of an event. If you don't believe me, try charging a separate rate for those who want to stay and hear the speaker. Those three students will really enjoy it!

But this brings up another issue: What if your budget demands a ticket price that's just too high? How do you lower it? In other words, what do you do if you need to charge a lot less? What if you need to cut out half your budget to match a reasonable income for expected numbers?

Good questions.

ONE WAY IS TO SIMPLY CUT ITEMS OF COST. But usually this is easier said than done. Many of these cuts may have consequences. For example, if you cut out the pizza, you only save $3 a kid and lose your biggest draw. It's not worth it.

What about the speaker? For some of us, $1000 plus travel expenses is a huge financial commitment. But if we cut the professional speaker and try to bring in an amateur, we may not accomplish our main purpose of sharing the gospel—the whole reason we're doing this event in the first place.

I remember looking for speakers when I ran a small weekly outreach. At the time, even $100 seemed like a lot to pay for a speaker. After all, I only had 30 or 40 students in a good week. Sometimes I was able to find some great starting speakers in my area who didn't mind speaking for a small honorarium. And realistically, for a weekly outreach we didn't have a huge need to book national speakers that we had to fly out and put up in a hotel. But as I teamed up with other youth ministries and partnered with five to 10 other groups for some events, we were able to bring out more students and increase our speaker budget. Before long we were bringing out bands and speakers that required a big chunk of our budget. But they were always worth it, if they helped us with our draw and our purpose.

We'll talk more about booking good speakers in chapter 10, but here's a good rule of thumb: You don't want to be cheap when you're booking the one person who's going to communicate the gospel to this kind of audience.

So how can we charge less if we can't afford to cut costs? Another option is to fund part of the event from the church budget. I've talked with numerous youth leaders who've approached their senior pastors with a vision for a community outreach. Once the church got involved—maybe even the missions committee—then the necessary funds were allocated toward the event. However, this can take time. Churches don't usually like to be asked for money for an event that's happening in just three weeks. Churches should be approached at least six months ahead of time or, ideally, at the beginning of the planning process.

Sometimes a number of churches will pitch in together to help fund events like these. I just spoke at a community-wide event in a very small town in Iowa where five different churches pitched in a few hundred dollars each. But this seed money was the beginning of a budget for the event. Multiple churches now owned the event together, and the cost of the tickets was much more affordable for teenagers.

You may try to acquire funding from your own church and from other area churches, but sometimes it just isn't possible and you still come up empty. Don't despair. You can always approach individual donors. I've done this frequently. I make a list of local Christian businessmen and families who have a heart for evangelism. Then I call them one at a time and ask them something like this:

> We have an event coming up, and I need your help. We're trying to bring in 300 students from the community and share the gospel with them. First of all, we need your prayers, but I'm also looking for financial sponsors. In order to attract this kind of crowd, our cover charge can't be too expensive. We've been prudent with our budgeting, but our admission price is still too high. I need to partner with 15 people who are willing to donate $100 to this event. This would make the event cost only $5 a kid, and it will attract more unchurched kids to the event. Would you like to be involved?

I've had a lot of success with this kind of request, and I've rarely missed my fundraising goal. These donors pray for the students, and we get back to each one of them with the results of the event. People love the opportunity to make a difference in the lives of teenagers.

Granted, you can't do this every month. This is the kind of request I make only once or twice a year. But these donations can keep expensive ticket costs from hindering your draw.

MONEY ISN'T YOUR ONLY NECESSARY RESOURCE. YOU ALSO NEED TO CONSIDER SUPPLIES AND WORKERS. Go over the event in your mind and write down every possible supply (whether you already have them or not) and every possible volunteer you'll need to help you on the day of the event. The lists for the LOL event example might look like this:

LOL EVENT SUPPLIES:

Sound System	ALREADY HAVE
Video Projector/Screen	BORROW
Lights	RENT SOME/ALREADY HAVE SOME
CDs or Music to Play	BORROW
Signs	MAKE OURSELVES
Tables	BORROW
Chairs/Seating	ALREADY HAVE
Prizes	BUY/HAVE DONATED
Response Cards	ALREADY HAVE
Pens/Pencils	ALREADY HAVE
Plates, Cups, and Napkins	BUY

LOL EVENT WORKERS:

Emcee

Speaker

30 Counselors

staring at a blank piece of paper

EMT/Nurse

Soundman

6 Registration Workers

12 Security Guards

ADVERTISING IS ABOUT MORE THAN JUST PRINTING FLYERS. Advertising begins when you plan your draw—the biggest advertising asset. Without a creative event title, pizza, prizes, and comedy elements, our LOL flyers would look pretty empty. It does no good to hang up a poster that teenagers merely look at and walk away. A well-thought-out draw makes advertising easier.

But a good draw isn't enough on its own. You still have to get the word out. One way to do this is through flyers, posters, and mailers. In addition, the Internet has opened up new opportunities to do this through sites like MySpace.com.

Consider radio advertising—and not just through the local Christian radio station. Remember your audience—teenagers who don't know Jesus. Find out what mainstream stations teenagers in your area listen to. I'll never forget hearing advertisements for a church youth group on a popular mainstream radio station. The ads were creative and funny, and I heard they yielded some pretty good results, too.

The best way to get the word out is by networking with other youth leaders. And don't limit yourself to just churches. Check to see if Youth for Christ, Young Life, Fellowship of Christian Athletes, or other "on campus" youth organizations are involved with students in the area. These groups can bring out a ton of unchurched youth. In chapter 9, "Programming Large Events," I'll share some more about the importance of networking and creating a committee of area youth leaders.

As effective as networking is, you shouldn't neglect going directly to your audience. If your purpose is to "reach unchurched kids for Christ," then don't just announce the event at youth group. Try to find a way to advertise directly on campus or in places where teens hang out in the area. Local teen centers, music stores, and video arcades might let you hang up posters. It never hurts to ask. And the Christian organizations mentioned previously can also be a big help with on-campus promotion. They usually have easy access to the campuses and know the guidelines about promoting events like these.

But sometimes on-campus promotion can be difficult, in which case your students will have the best access to marketing the event on campus. So encourage churches to send their teenagers to certain campuses with flyers and promotional materials, while still respecting the guidelines and going through the proper channels.

Events like our LOL example create even more advertising avenues, such as the video contest. You'll have to promote a contest like that well ahead of the event if you want to get people involved. Thus, promoting the video contest will also promote the larger event.

Don't underestimate the power of the "word of mouth." If you provide a great draw and give your students the initiative to spread the word, the news will travel. Get churches to provide incentives like prizes for students who bring the most friends to the event. You can even reward the churches or groups who bring the most students.

The key to advertising is providing an attractive draw and then communicating this to as many teenagers as possible, as many times as possible.

6. Plan Your Program Agenda

So now it seems you're almost finished with the planning process. You've already done the following:

1. Pray: Give this program or event to God and bring him into the planning process at the beginning so it's his program, not your program.

2. Plan Your Purpose: Know the goal of your program or event. What end result are you shooting for? If this is an outreach program, then your goal is to *reach out to those who don't know Jesus and point them toward him*. Everything you do with this program must help you achieve this goal.

3. Pinpoint Your Target Audience: Determine who you want to draw to this program. With outreach programs, remember you're drawing those who don't know Jesus, but also consider what age you'll target, what region, and maybe even more specifics.

4. Brainstorm Your Draw: What will bring your target students to this program or event? Your purpose isn't enough. You need to get them there.

5. Consider Your Resources: You need to consider your budget, your need for supplies and workers, and a plan for advertising. This step really helps you dive into the specifics of your program or event, evaluating what's feasible and what's just wishful thinking. It also provides you with rough budgets, supply lists, and worker lists.

Getting through all of the above steps is huge. But you're not finished yet. What are you going to do when all the students show up? What will the event actually look like? How long should you allocate for each element?

These are all great questions. That's why we're talking about "what" happens "when" in the next chapter.

"what" happens "when"
planning our program agenda

The event was an absolute catastrophe. Afterward the students left feeling duped, and the people who ran it vowed never to do another one. And it was all because of the *program agenda*.

The event started to fall apart an hour before it even began. The event planners had set up a registration table manned by two sweet little old ladies, but they never thought about when the students would be let inside the facility. The first few students asked what they should do once they'd registered, and the ladies replied, "Go inside, I guess."

And what would the teenagers do once they were inside? Would there be music playing? Would there be something playing on the video screens? The planners also never thought through how the program would actually start. Would someone stand up and welcome the students, or would the band just start playing?

As it turned out, students entered a quiet room filled with nothing but chairs and a stage. The atmosphere was dull; and before long, teenagers were wandering the halls looking for something to do until the "program" started. Bob and Lester, two adult volunteers who'd been given security badges five minutes prior, were running around like border collies trying to herd students back inside.

The program started about 10 minutes late because the event coordinators were running around trying to solve other unexpected problems. And when the emcee finally took the stage, it was very evident that he was talking to the wrong audience. He took about 10 minutes to do the welcome and told everyone how excited he was that the event had come together. No one cared—no one in the room anyway. Anyone who'd helped plan the event was outside the room helping Bob and Lester collect students from the hallways and sidewalks and attempting to detour them back into the main auditorium.

Some students never made it back inside. The word had already spread: "This stinks!" So they hooked up with their friends and decided to do something else with their Saturday night. The event had barely started, yet it was already spiraling out of control.

FAILING TO PLAN "WHAT" HAPPENS "WHEN"

The event's organizers had made a common mistake. They'd "planned"—but they'd also "failed to plan." What? While they planned the logistics down to the last detail, they just whipped out the "program agenda." In other words, they did most of the things we talked about in the last chapter, but then they stopped. They never planned "what" would happen "when." Often we spend so much time planning all the logistics of an event that we have a false sense of security, and we believe everything is prepared. But if our "program agenda" isn't laid out in detail, then all is wasted.

In the last chapter, you planned all the essential logistics of your LOL event: Purpose, draw, budget, supplies and workers, and marketing. These five elements are all crucial, and to the untrained eye it seems like everything is accounted for.

"what" happens "when"

Not quite.

Now it's time to put together a program agenda—our guide to "what" happens "when."

PUTTING IT ON PAPER

Sounds easy. We've already done all the brainstorming, acquired a facility, recruited workers, solicited prizes, and arranged to fly out a speaker. What's left? Just transposing those elements to a piece of paper under the title PROGRAM AGENDA, right?

That's what the group in the above example did for their event, and the results were heartbreaking. It was a three-and-a-half hour event, and they'd lined up two bands and a speaker who was supposed to give two talks. They'd also included a break in the middle of it all. Not a bad layout—I've seen similar agendas work just fine.

Here was their event itinerary as it looked on paper:

Program Agenda

7:00	Concert #1
7:45	Speaker
8:30	Break for Snacks/Give Away Prizes
9:15	Concert #2
9:45	Speaker—Session 2
10:15	Band—Closing Songs
10:30	Event Ends

It's not the simplest of programs, I'll admit; but it doesn't look like anything is missing. The majority of "youth rallies" have just one band and one speaking session. This event just required more transitions, more set up, more preparation, and more planning. In other words, it's a good example for us to practice with. If we can plan this event successfully, future events may be even easier to program.

So what's wrong with this program agenda? Why did it turn into such a nightmare? Look at it again. As a rough outline, there's nothing wrong with it. But it's not detailed enough for a program agenda. It's a great start; we just need to fill in the missing elements.

THE 25 QUESTIONS

When I looked at this agenda, a few questions immediately came to mind—25 to be exact. If you look at the agenda carefully, you'll have questions, too. Just go through the event in your mind, and soon all of the missing elements will begin to rear their ugly heads. During the planning process, we

"what" happens "when"

always need to begin asking ourselves questions about the event, starting at the very beginning.

Here were my immediate questions from the above agenda:

1. What time will students arrive and register/check in/pay?

2. When will we let them in the room?

3. What will be going on in the room while students arrive and take their seats?

4. What video, sound, and lighting will be needed to help during this time?

5. How will everyone know when the program is beginning?

6. Who will emcee?

7. How will we start the evening?

8. Who will introduce the band?

9. How long will the band *really* play (once you add time for all this other stuff)?

10. Who will introduce the speaker?

11. How long will the speaker *really* talk?

12. Do we need time for an altar call?

13. Do we need time for counseling after the altar call?

14. What will happen after the altar call?

15. Who will give instructions about the break?

16. What will students do during the break?

17. How will we get students back from the break?

18. How are we going to give away prizes during the break?

19. When will the second band set up and do a sound check?

20. Who will introduce the second band?

21. How long will the second band play?

22. Who will introduce the speaker the second time?

23. How will we transition from the speaker's second session to the final songs of the band?

24. Who will close the event?

25. What will be going on while the students are leaving?

Planning with this amount of detail is essential. If you don't do it, your entire program agenda will suffer. Some of these questions will have quick, easy answers. Others will take time and planning to figure out.

Unfortunately, the above group never took time to consider these vital details and their event was disastrous. It's not because they were bad people. They were great people who really loved Jesus. They just didn't know how to plan a detailed agenda.

I already shared the difficulties this group had just starting the event. Once it finally started—it only got worse.

WHAT ACTUALLY HAPPENED

Once the emcee got going, he thanked everyone who helped make the event happen: Marge, for preparing the snacks in the kitchen; Curly and all the other guys from Rosemont Presbyterian for setting up the chairs; and so on. There was jaded applause. Then he announced there'd be a break at 8:30 and that's when they'd give away the prizes—a bunch of students looked at the clock on the wall, obviously wishing it was already 8:30.

The event just snowballed from there—and it was all downhill. (As you read on, refer to the original agenda that follows to see how much the program strayed from the original plan.)

Original Program Agenda

7:00	Concert #1
7:45	Speaker
8:30	Break for snacks/give away prizes
9:15	Concert #2
9:45	Speaker—Session 2
10:15	Band—Closing songs
10:30	Event ends

Concert #1 at 7 PM? Not quite. After all the announcements

and thank yous, the band was introduced at 7:21. So much for the 45-minute set they'd planned. But no worries for them, they played for 42 minutes, ending at 8:03—exactly 18 minutes after the speaker was supposed to get onstage.

The speaker was supposed to be done by 8:30. He was close. He gave an altar call at 8:36. But that took seven minutes, and then the counselors prayed with the students for another 10 minutes. The first band returned to the stage during the altar call and felt "led" to play another worship song after the students had finished praying. I guess they were "led" not to give the students a break when promised.

The emcee finally popped up at 8:57 and dismissed 300 angry students 27 minutes late for their break. But at least he told the students they didn't need to be back until 9:30, giving them a 12-minute shorter break than planned, and pushing everything back until 9:30.

The second band wasn't happy when they were asked to cut three songs to try to make up for the time lost. In the end, they agreed to cut two numbers, and they promised to hurry. But they were too busy to argue, as they were also trying to set up their equipment—and all in less than 30 minutes. It wasn't happening!

That was the least of the event coordinators' problems. Unfortunately, they couldn't get everyone back from the break by 9:30. The PA system in the fellowship hall wasn't that loud, and everyone was too spread out. Security and other event volunteers roamed the halls trying to herd the kids back inside, but—let's just say lots of students suddenly had to go to the bathroom. So the prize giveaways didn't happen as planned.

The emcee took the stage at about 9:38 and welcomed most of the audience back. (Approximately 30 students were still unaccounted for.) While the band was trying to get their last few cords plugged in, the emcee drew names for a few of

"what" happens "when"

the prizes, including the most coveted: A brand new TV/DVD combo.

The band was quickly introduced at 9:46, exactly one minute after they were scheduled to be finished. Regaining their composure, they talked for three minutes about how they didn't have time to set up all their equipment, but they'd try their best to perform. They played a 25-minute set, including the three-minute speech, feeling pretty honorable since they were supposed to have a 30-minute set. The band left the stage and the speaker was introduced at 10:12, exactly three minutes before he was supposed to be done. He cut his 30-minute talk to 26 minutes. Three groups left in the middle of his opening prayer. One group stopped and apologized at the door: "Sorry, but we told parents we'd be back at 11:00."

The band came up to start their final set eight minutes after the event was supposed to be over. But the event finally did end. Not just for the evening—forever.

It's a shame this event turned out the way it did, because it really wasn't missing much. The planners had lined up good talent and an effective speaker. But it was disorganized. It was like watching a football team that had never practiced together "show up" at the Super Bowl and hope for the best.

The real tragedy is in the fact that most unchurched kids will *not* come back to events or programs that give a bad first impression. And it's likely we'll lose more than just those students who experienced the failed event firsthand. They'll tell all their friends how "lame" it was, too. If we give teenagers a bad first impression, "word of mouth" can actually work against us.

How could they have programmed this event better? The event needed a realistic program agenda.

FOUR PROGRAM AGENDA ESSENTIALS

I've found four program agenda essentials that have helped greatly over the years. These four steps may also help you as you take all your logistical planning from chapter 5 and turn it into a detailed program agenda.

Let's make the above program more realistic. In doing this, you'll learn the essentials of planning your future program agendas. (These essentials can also apply to weekly programs, but we'll go over more specific "weekly program" details in chapter 8.)

Here are the four steps for planning a realistic program agenda:

1. Lay Out a Rough Outline

Sometimes this will require more brainstorming. Think through the ramifications of *what* happens *when*. Should the speaker go first or should the band? How long should the event last and when should you offer a break? If you give away prizes, when should that happen? How can you keep students interested until the end of the program? These are all important things to consider.

There are some basic rules to follow when you're laying out your rough program agenda:

> • From the very beginning, the audience should
> be happy to be there. During the first 30 seconds
> after students sit down for a program, they're asking
> themselves, "Is this going to stink or what?" Answer
> that question with an unarguable "NO!" right away.
>
> • Get the audience involved immediately. Don't let
> them sit there and get bored. Make them hesitate

"what" happens "when"

before they even head to the bathroom, for fear they'll miss something spectacular.

• Get the audience used to looking and listening up front. Have something entertaining onstage that captivates their attention. You don't want to create a coffeehouse environment where teenagers are sitting and talking with their friends, while treating the stage entertainment as background music.

• Transitions, transitions, transitions! Create a smooth segue from your activities to your speaker! Don't allow a lengthy "dead time" between acts. Don't give students a chance to tune out because "the fun's over and the speaker has begun!"

Consider these rules and ramifications while you're laying out your rough outline on paper. I can't provide you with one basic model or layout of what these types of outlines should look like because all programs are different. But here are several examples of rough outlines, just to give you the basic idea:

Youth Fest

7:00	Band 1
7:45	Band 2
8:20	Speaker
8:50	Door Prizes
9:00	Close

Skate Town

2:00	Skateboarding
5:00	Dinner/Skate Events Still Open
6:00	Skate Demo
6:20	Testimony
6:30	Speaker
7:00	More Skateboarding
8:00	Close

Three on Three

3:00	Three-on-Three Tournaments/ Concession Stand Open
7:00	Award Ceremony Begins—Celebrity Guest Testimony
7:30	Give Out Awards
8:00	Close

"what" happens "when"

Winter Xtremz

7:00	Inflatables, Carnival Activities
10:00	Close Down Activities/Break Dance Team Onstage
10:15	Crowd Game
10:20	Up Front Game with Four Students Onstage
10:30	Speaker
11:00	Close

If you're not exactly sure how to lay out your basic agenda, you can model your program after a similar one you've seen or attended before. You can also ask others who've done similar programming to share a format they've used in the past.

You'll notice that several of the latter "agendas" have beginning activities that take up hours of the event. In the case of "Skate Town," "Three on Three," and "Winter Xtremz," the programs don't really begin until after the initial hours of the main activity. So when I plan "Winter Xtremz," the program portion of the event doesn't start until 10 at night. I have to make sure I have everything organized down to the last detail from 7 PM to 10 PM, but my "program" portion of the event doesn't start until 10. That's when I need to figure out how to get 1,000 ADHD junior highers off my inflatables and over to the stage area to listen to my speaker.

Regardless of what it looks like, we need to get the rough outline on paper. That's what the group at the beginning of this chapter did. Unfortunately, they stopped there and never worked out the details.

How do we identify the details that need working out? Let's go on to step two.

2. Play 25 Questions

This is where the fun begins. Try to come up with at least 25 questions about your rough outline and use these to identify any "holes" in the program. You saw the 25 I came up with earlier in this chapter. I just start with the beginning of the event and work through the outline in chronological order. My first questions will almost always be about when the students arrive— how they'll register, how and when they'll get into the room, and what kinds of preshow preparations need to be made. These questions also get you thinking about your time schedule before the actual program. You can't just start your agenda with "7:00—Concert." If you don't think through registration and preshow, chaos begins before the program even launches.

Once you have the beginning worked out, keep asking questions about the program itself. If there's a band, ask yourself if they're going to walk onstage, or whether someone will introduce them. How will you get from the band to the speaker portion of the event? If there's a break, how will you get the students back from the break? These questions need to continue all the way through the end of the program.

When you've asked every possible question you can think of, it's time for the next essential step in planning your program agenda.

3. Answer and Adjust

Now you must answer each one of your questions and adjust your agenda with the new times and information you've come up with.

To do this, let's look at my initial 25 questions above. I'll answer each question and then we'll create a new "adjusted" program agenda below.

25 QUESTIONS: ANSWERED AND ADJUSTED

1. WHAT TIME WILL STUDENTS ARRIVE AND REGISTER/CHECK IN/ PAY? Don't just write down the start time of the event. You need to plan for when students arrive and registration begins. This needs to be on your agenda. You also want to have some sort of card for them to fill out at registration so you can contact them about future events. If your event is big, you'll want more than one check-in table with alphabetical lines to make the registration process easy for students. If you offered a "preregistration" or "group registration" option, have tables set up for those as well. Have a game plan in case 300 students show up five minutes before the event.

2. WHEN WILL WE LET THEM IN THE ROOM? Always note what time the doors will open. This way you can plan accordingly for your preprogram, which is what originally led me to my next question.

3. WHAT WILL BE GOING ON IN THE ROOM WHILE STUDENTS ARRIVE AND TAKE THEIR SEATS? Here lies your preprogram. What can you do to create a fun atmosphere and entertain students while they take their seats? This might be as simple as playing loud music. But don't stop there. Why not play some sports videos or funny bloopers on a big screen onstage? Maybe launch a few giant beach balls into the crowd and get those batted around.

4. WHAT VIDEO, SOUND, AND LIGHTING WILL BE NEEDED TO HELP DURING THIS TIME? Most programs require some sort of audio-visual equipment. You might as well use this stuff for your preprogram as well. Teenagers like darkened rooms with flashing lights and loud music. And a video element will get them used to focusing on the stage where the action will be taking place during most of the night.

5. HOW WILL EVERYONE KNOW WHEN THE PROGRAM IS BEGINNING? I like to display a countdown. I literally have a clock counting backward on the video screen(s) from five minutes until start time. (www.SimplyYouthMinistry.com sells some of these.) Every minute someone uses their best monster truck rally announcer's voice to say that the program will start "in four minutes…," "in three minutes…," until finally at one minute we kill all the lights and start rolling spotlights across the crowd. When 10 seconds remain, a voice begins counting down out loud, and the crowd always joins in. At zero—the program begins!

6. WHO WILL EMCEE? I use almost as much caution when I'm choosing an emcee as I do when I'm choosing a speaker. An emcee can really make or break an event. I like choosing someone who'll connect with my audience verbally and visually. Student speakers can be effective, but only if they're very sharp and not intimidated by speaking into a mic in front of a crowd.

7. HOW WILL WE START THE EVENING? Whatever you do, don't stand up and start thanking everyone who made the event possible. Remember your audience. They don't care about Marge in the kitchen. Save your thanks for after the event. Just get this thing rolling! At this particular event, they could have had the emcee take the stage at the end of the countdown.

With a lot of energy, he could have yelled, "Welcome to (insert the name of the event)!" They could have tossed T-shirts or prizes into the audience. Or it could have started with the band kicking right into their first song with no talk at all. The less talk the better, actually. But we'll assume that for this event we have a really good emcee. For the new agenda below, we'll have the emcee do the welcome, and we'll also include T-shirt launchers.

8. WHO WILL INTRODUCE THE BAND? In this event, the countdown voice could have just said, "Ladies and Gentleman, let's give a warm welcome to—" and introduced the band. If not, the emcee could quickly do it. As we said above, we'll just have the emcee do it.

9. HOW LONG WILL THE BAND REALLY PLAY (ONCE YOU ADD TIME FOR ALL THIS OTHER STUFF)? If this group had planned a preprogram and started the countdown on time, the first band could have had a full 45 minutes. But let's do some calculations. Personally, I would have probably started the five-minute countdown at 7 PM because youth groups are habitually late. Then the "zero" would arrive at 7:05, and the band would begin, giving them a true 30- to 40-minute set. Most bands will appreciate less time, if they've been told the time limit from the beginning. For our revised agenda, we'll have the emcee come on at 7:05 after the five-minute countdown. We'll also have him introduce the band by 7:08. I don't know how long the band gets to play yet. I need to look forward in the agenda at the speaker and figure out how much time she needs. Once we figure that out, we can calculate how much time to give the band.

10. WHO WILL INTRODUCE THE SPEAKER? The band could introduce the speaker. Or if you have a good emcee, he could do it. Plan your time schedule down to the minute. If there are any announcements or logistics that need to be announced, consider putting them off until later. This is the most important transition of the evening, and you don't want to lose students at this point—so don't give them even a five-second pause to exit. We'll have the emcee introduce our speaker.

11. How long will the speaker really talk? In the agenda above, the speaker was supposed to start at 7:45 and end at 8:30. If we need the speaker to stop at 8:30, then we need to work backward from this point. But first we need to answer some more questions before we calculate how long the speaker will talk.

12. Do we need time for an altar call? If you're going to do an altar call, then you'll need to plan for it. In this case, we could have the speaker talk for just 30 minutes, do a five-minute altar call, and then give 10 or 15 minutes for counselors to pray with any teenagers who come forward. If you aren't going to do an altar call, are you going to have the teenagers who make decisions raise their hands? Are you going to have them fill out response cards? Who will pass out those cards? Will they have pens or pencils? How will you collect them? For this event we'll send them out with counselors. That led me to the next question.

13. Do we need time for counseling after the altar call? If you decide to do an altar call where you want to send students out of the room to meet with counselors, then you need to do two things: 1) Plan at least 15 minutes for this part, 2) Plan something for the rest of the audience to do. And you don't want this to be something too desirable, because you don't want students *not* to come forward because they don't want to miss something cool. Usually, if I had a band present, I'd just let them play a few more numbers while some students are out of the room with the counselors. If there's no band, you can lead a few crowd games.

So we're finally at the point where we can calculate the band's ending time and the speaker's start time. Begin at our 8:30 break and work backward. This is a great programming concept I learned years ago. Often, our most important programming elements are at the end. If our purpose was

"what" happens "when"

"sharing the gospel," then our program might very likely include altar calls and counseling time. By programming backward, you can get in the important things first. Then as you work backward, you can block out the time needed for each of these important elements.

At this event we want to do an altar call, and we know we need to allow 15 minutes for it. That means we need to be sending students out of the room with counselors no later than 8:15. But the actual altar call takes five minutes. So our speaker needs to start inviting students forward at 8:10.

I want to give the speaker 30 minutes of speaking time, so I'll have my speaker come on at 7:40. That means our first band needs to finish their set at 7:40 (finally, the answer to question #9). Then the emcee will stand up and give a 15-second introduction for the speaker.

14. WHAT WILL HAPPEN AFTER THE ALTAR CALL? Since the first band's set was cut to just 32 minutes, they're going to be thrilled to come back up during the altar call. We'll have the band play an additional 15-minute set starting at 8:15 during the counseling time. Then I'd dismiss everyone to the break promptly at 8:30, having counselors dismiss the students they counsel straight to the break.

15. WHO WILL GIVE INSTRUCTIONS ABOUT THE BREAK? The emcee. This brought up my next question.

16. WHAT WILL STUDENTS DO DURING THE BREAK? I would provide snacks and then set up some sort of sound system in the snack area so I could play music and create a cool atmosphere to just hang out. Teenagers like to hang out.

17. HOW WILL WE GET STUDENTS BACK FROM THE BREAK? This is one of the best questions we can ask. Whenever we have students roaming around, and we want them to congregate somewhere at a certain time, we need to think of incentives. That's why we spend so much attention on preprogram, to initially get them in the main auditorium and keep them there. Now we need to think similarly about how we'll get them back inside.

First, tape off areas where you don't want teenagers to wander off. You can use yellow caution tape and funny signs like "Danger, Rabid Squirrel Crossing! Do Not Enter!" Post security people in key areas to make sure students don't venture off-limits.

Second, provide incentives to get them back in the auditorium. In this particular event we can kill the music in the snack area about 10 minutes before the program begins and launch the music in the main auditorium again. We'll keep announcing the start time in both rooms. Launch the countdown in the main room five minutes before the start time.

We have even more incentives to get students back in the room. Luckily, we have prizes to give away—which brings me to my next question.

18. HOW ARE WE GOING TO GIVE AWAY PRIZES DURING THE BREAK? Don't. This idea was a mistake to begin with. Don't give away prizes during a break. Instead, use them as leverage to get students back inside the main auditorium on time. I would have scheduled a 30-minute break, and then I'd get students back at 9 PM, allocating about 10 minutes to give away prizes from the main stage. When the emcee dismisses students for the break at 8:30, he can announce, "Don't forget to be back here at nine o'clock! We'll be giving away the TV/DVD player at nine o'clock sharp!"

19. WHEN WILL THE SECOND BAND SET UP? Most bands couldn't set up and do a sound check during a 30-minute break. And really, they'd only have 20 minutes because you want to start bringing students into the room again 10 minutes before the program resumes. So either the second band would have to share equipment with the first band, or you'd have to use only one band that would play two sets. Bands share stages in clubs all the time. They usually share drum sets, and then they set up their other stuff, covering it with black sheets. We'll assume the bands can share equipment for our agenda below. (Obviously, they can do quick swaps of guitars, etc., but we won't try to switch out any sound, drums, or lighting.)

20. WHO WILL INTRODUCE THE SECOND BAND? The emcee, after the prizes are distributed.

21. HOW LONG WILL THE SECOND BAND PLAY? Now that we have everything on schedule, they'd be able to play a full 30 minutes as planned.

22. WHO WILL INTRODUCE THE SPEAKER THE SECOND TIME? I would just have the band introduce her for a quick transition. Why risk losing students' attention while an emcee comes up, only to turn around and reintroduce the speaker? Transitions are key! But be aware: I've seen *numerous* bands forget to do the intro. You have to clearly communicate and remind the band that they're introducing the speaker. Maybe have the emcee stand ready on one side of the stage—just in case the band forgets.

23. HOW WILL WE TRANSITION FROM THE SPEAKER'S SECOND SESSION TO THE FINAL SONGS OF THE BAND? I would have the band come up during the prayer. We won't be doing a second altar call.

24. WHO WILL CLOSE THE EVENT? I would have the emcee say a few final words and announce the date of next year's event!

25. WHAT WILL BE GOING ON WHILE THE STUDENTS ARE LEAVING? As the emcee says the final goodbye, I'd start playing loud music again or let the band play an instrumental for the exit.

So now the same program, with just some fine-tuning on the agenda, could look like this:

Adjusted Program Agenda

6:00	Registration begins
6:30	**Doors open (lights are dim, loud music, skating/BMX videos)**
6:45	Beach balls (volunteers launch giant beach balls into the crowd)
6:55	Voice announces that the program begins in 10 minutes (start showing blooper videos with some sound, drawing more attention to the stage)
7:00	Countdown begins (lights flash in the lobby, voice on the PA announces start time every minute, start 5-minute countdown video)
7:04	1-minute countdown (lights go dark, rolling spotlights, countdown video continues; at 10 seconds monster-truck voice counts down every second)
7:05	EMCEE: "Welcome to _____" (10 helpers run out and throw T-shirts into the audience)
7:07	**EMCEE introduces the FIRST BAND**
7:40	**EMCEE introduces the SPEAKER**
8:10	Speaker gives altar call
8:15	**Kids leave for counseling/band plays**

"what" happens "when"

8:30	**EMCEE announces the break (important: be back at 9:00 for drawing of TV/DVD)**

BREAK (snacks, music, watch doors—no in-and-out privileges)

8:50	Doors open in the main room again (kill music in the break area, begin music in the main room)
8:55	Begin five-minute countdown (loud music, another countdown video)
8:59	One-minute countdown (lights go dark, rolling spotlights, countdown video continues; at 10 seconds monster-truck voice counts down every second)
9:00	EMCEE welcomes everyone back. Give away prizes. When finished with prizes, shoot some more T-shirts into the audience
9:15	**EMCEE introduces SECOND BAND, which uses the same equipment as the first for Concert #2**
9:45	**Second Band introduces SPEAKER for Session 2**
10:15	**Band comes up during the prayer (closing songs)**
10:30	EMCEE: "See ya next year!" (loud music and full house lights)

Which event would you want to attend?

Yes, this event would require a little more preparation. We'd need to find those skating/BMX videos and prepare the countdowns with all the right music. We'd need to find T-shirt launchers or recruit some people to help us throw them into the audience. Good programming of our "program agenda" will make us return to our "workers" and "supplies" lists and add new items.

But basically, the program we modified is NOT much different than the original. It's just organized to remember every detail, to be more realistic with time, and to always consider our audience. Because of this, the result seems like an entirely different event.

WHAT IF THINGS TAKE LONGER THAN PLANNED?

You'll notice that I have certain times in boldface in our new agenda. Those bold items represent key elements of our program. Every single item is important; but with a glance, I want to be able to see when the doors open, the program begins, the band starts, the speaker starts, and so on.

If you run behind, then you have to adjust on the fly. This becomes easier as you gain more programming experience. You won't panic if the band takes eight minutes too long. You just look at the big picture and see what can be adjusted and what can't. Maybe you'll cut three minutes from the speaker and go to break just five minutes late. Cutting the speaker should be the last resort if he's sharing the gospel. But you'll learn to look at your agenda, see what needs to be cut, and make those calls. The more events you do, the more you'll accurately predict the times and equip the participants to stick to them.

But let's do one more step, just to be sure we didn't miss anything.

4. Use Six Eyes

Review your program agenda again with two more people. Now is the time to notice mistakes—not the night of the program. I prefer to have several minds working together on the programming process. I like to have at least two others with me when I put together my program agenda. Sometimes one person will pick up on an item that others totally missed.

Even if you've involved others in the original planning process, get at least two new sets of eyes to look at your adjusted program agenda and see if they can come up with any questions. Don't argue with their questions, just write them down. Go through the process again and see if their observations are valid.

I've done this process before only to realize that I forgot huge elements of a program.

"When are they going to eat the pizza?"

"DOH!"

Don't hesitate to involve others in the process. Six eyes are better than two.

WHAT ABOUT THE HOLY SPIRIT?

Some people would say that this kind of planning doesn't leave room for the Holy Spirit. Is God really so confined by time and space?

I was at a recent event where the person in charge was going over the time schedule with the band. The band was last and they were supposed to finish at 11 PM.

The lead singer said, "We'll shoot for 11 o'clock, but we'll see what the Spirit leads us to do."

The event planner paused for a second and thought about it. But then she commented, "Well, I know many of the churches attending have told parents they'll be back at a certain time. And some of these churches have quite a drive ahead of them. We need to respect that."

The lead singer of the band simply retorted, "Well, if the Spirit is leading us to pray with kids and minister to them, I don't think we should worry about time. After all, groups can just leave if they really have to."

The event leader paused for a moment again. She finally pulled the leader of the band aside. "I really appreciate your desire to minister. But the fact is, we've rented this high school and told them we'd be out by a certain time. The janitors are right over there waiting for us to be finished. And frankly, they're a little skeptical of us." She went on, "We told churches the event will be over at 11 PM, which is a little late already, and they've made plans for transportation. If you look out in the parking lot, next to all the church vans and personal vehicles, you'll notice two charter buses. Those buses charge by the hour. I'm not going to make churches have to pay more." She paused for a second and looked at some of her volunteers standing around the room. "And I told my volunteers they'd be home by a certain time. When I say something, I keep my word. And I don't think the Spirit is leading me to break that, so you need to be off the stage at 11."

Sometimes we blame the Holy Spirit for our own laziness. Don't throw around the phrase "Let's see what the Spirit leads us to do" as an excuse for not planning.

The Holy Spirit will lead you when you plan. God was with us since the beginning of the event. We started the planning of this event in prayer, and he'll continue to guide us throughout the event.

And I promise you, the Holy Spirit won't lead you to break your word or break a contract. If you feel the Spirit's leading to keep the agenda open at the end, then by all means, leave it open. Put it on all your flyers, "7 PM—until we finish!" Rent the facility until well past the time the event would require. There's nothing wrong with this, but don't let it stifle you from planning all the intricate details and fun extras that help your event achieve its purpose.

IT AIN'T OVER 'TIL IT'S OVER

Our event isn't completely planned until the program agenda has been laid out down to the last minute. Don't neglect this crucial four-step process we've just reviewed. Go through the entire program in your mind and on paper. Ask questions about every detail. Go through the program again with others and implore them to ask questions and search for holes

This attention to detail might appear obsessive-compulsive or a little stringent. It's not. It's just good programming. *Meticulous* can sometimes be interpreted as a bad word. Yet God himself was meticulous with his creation and in his instructions to us throughout history. Have you ever looked at a snowflake? Have you ever rubbed your fingers across the surface of a rose or seen the detail in the color of a Monarch butterfly? What about God's instructions to Solomon for how to build God's temple? When people gazed upon the results of God's design, *meticulous* was far from being a bad word.

This kind of attention to detail also makes good programming. It will introduce new creative elements into the program, and it will assure smoother transitions. Without it, we'll be playing catch-up all night, possibly leaving a wake of frustration for everyone involved and in attendance.

programming on-campus outreach clubs

student- and adult-led campus ministry programming

The bell rings and students fill the hallways of the overcrowded suburban junior high school. In only five minutes, half the students will be in their next classrooms, and the other half will fill the quad and the cafeteria for what this school calls "A-lunch."

But this particular Friday is a little different. Approximately 50 to 60 students have found their way to an overcrowded classroom for a student-led event called "Escape," which is held on the first Friday of every month.

Today, "Escape" is offering all-you-can-eat pizza and all-you-can-drink sodas for just $2. It's only 30 minutes long, and students say it's always fun. Food, fun activities, usually someone giving a short talk—and it's all student-led. This year 13 students gave their lives to Christ through this junior high program facilitated by a local youth pastor and his student leadership team.

Across the country it's three hours later. The bell rings and school is out for the day. High school students burst out of classrooms and head to the parking lots, bus stops, and the gym for practice. At 4:30 when all the sports activities end, loud music is pumping through the sound system in the band room. Athletes begin to congregate toward the music. They're soon joined by other students who've returned to the campus for this weekly Wednesday night program that students know as Young Life.

Adult youth workers greet students amidst the pounding of the subwoofers. Students hang out, eventually filling the room by 4:50 when the doors are closed. Three students compete up front for a goofy prize, while the rest of the students laugh and cheer. A quick video clip is shown, and then students divide into small groups where they share their opinions and their hearts. The adult small group leaders share God's truth in each small group. Over 20 high school students gave their lives to Christ this year. Two-thirds of them are going to a local church now.

Three hundred miles south, about 30 high school students pack into the basement of a student named Brian who lives just down the street from the high school. This "campus club" doesn't actually meet on campus because the school never allowed it. But that didn't stop a couple of youth workers with a heart to reach the local campus. They met a few students from the area high school at a nearby Starbucks. After getting to know these teenagers a little better, the youth workers told the students about this fun thing called Campus Life.

The next week five students crowded into a Taco Bell booth, and the youth workers told them about all the fun things Campus Life does every year: Camping trips, weekend retreats, crazy events, and Wednesday nights in Brian's basement. Teenagers exit the restaurant that night with flyers that promise "Free root beer floats next Wednesday night in Brian's basement!"

When the next Wednesday arrives, 13 students show up for free root beer floats. They're invited back for more fun the next week when 19 students show up, and then 25 students the next. Before they know it, about 30 students show up to this outreach program every week. Seven students become Christians the first year, and four of them are from the original group in that Taco Bell booth.

All of the above examples are campus outreach programs: Two on campus, one off; one during school, two after school; one student-led (in junior high—can you believe it?) and two adult-led; one church-driven, two parachurch-driven. Although they look very different in location and format, they all achieve the same purpose: *Reaching out to the students from a particular campus who don't know Jesus.*

You may feel God leading you to start a ministry reaching out to a local campus. That's great. The local high school and junior high campuses are excellent mission fields.

But how do you know what type of program you should try? Should you do an on-campus or off-campus program? Should it be student-led or adult-led? What should the weekly format look like?

These are great questions—very similar to the questions that a woman named Amanda asked me in an e-mail a couple of years ago:

> Jonathan,
>
> My husband and I are youth pastors at our church and we really want to do more on-campus ministry. I was reading about a youth pastor who held a weekly pizza lunch at the local high school. I was wondering how to go about getting permission to do this. Who do you contact, and is it allowed?
>
> God bless,
>
> —Amanda, Roseville, California

Like Amanda, you may be wondering how to get something like this started.

REMEMBER YOUR PURPOSE

Don't forget your purpose. I've said it numerous times in these pages already, and I'll say it again: You need to decide which direction you're going to go before getting into it. And you need all your volunteers and ministry partners to be on the same page.

Campus ministries can have several different purposes. Bible clubs tend to focus on providing a place of growth for Christians. But if you're reading this book, you know we're talking about the goal or purpose of outreach. So you don't want to create a Bible club that only Christians want to attend. You want to draw non-Christian teenagers and share Christ with them.

Since your purpose is outreach and your target students are "outreach kids," you should think of a cool name—not "Bible Club" or "Christian Youth Club." Think about it. If you were an unchurched kid, would you want to attend something called "Bible Club" or "Christian Club"? Probably not.

You could call it "The Safehouse," a place where students are safe to have fun and share who they are. Or "The Rock"—solid ground when your world is shaky. You get the idea.

WHERE

Next, you should check out possible locations. Even if you think "on-campus" is the best option, you may not be able to get access to the campus. Many schools don't let ministries on campus either during or after school hours. In the United States, there isn't much you can do to fight this and, frankly, you don't want to fight it. Even if you win, you lose. You don't want the school administration against you. It would be better to run the ministry off-campus than to have pledged war against the very gatekeepers of the students we're trying to reach.

Schools don't have to let pastors on campus. The only hard-and-fast rule is that students can start a Bible club if other student clubs are allowed on campus (the equal access law). But that's a student-led club. And churches or religious organizations can rent school facilities in the same way that Boy Scouts or the local women's knitting club can. But these wouldn't be school-sponsored activities.

If schools *do* allow adults on campus, the normal stipulation is "don't proselytize," which is really just a fancy way of saying, "Don't talk about God." Don't knock it—it's a fair rule. If schools didn't do this, picture the campus: Buddhists, Hindus, Mormons, you name it—all walking around campus and pushing their religion. Campus holy wars! So if a school *does* allow youth workers on campus, they most often require us not to push our own programs or religion, but to simply be a positive example to the students. Very often you may have to go through the hoops of a TB test, getting fingerprinted, and so on. But at least you're allowed access to campus so you can build relationships with students.

How Can We Get on Campus

Sometimes it takes years to get access to a school campus. When I worked for Youth for Christ/Campus Life years ago, I tried to get onto a certain junior high campus for years with no luck. The principal always said he couldn't allow us on campus because of the "church and state thing." And he really didn't want to discuss the issue. So I ran an off-campus club by default, and just visited students on campus at graduations, football games, and school plays.

During these years I never raised a fuss—I didn't want to make the school an enemy. I just kept ministering to students, taking every opportunity to build good rapport—with the parents, too. Over the years I met numerous parents and community leaders, and eventually two of these parents ended up on the school board.

A few years later when a new principal took over, one of those board members introduced me to him, and I was on campus the next week. They not only gave me free access to the gym for our weekly program on Wednesday nights, but they also allowed our group to come on campus during the day. We could visit students during lunch period, as long as we didn't talk about God. But we could invite them to our Campus Life club in the school gym on Wednesday nights. This was a huge help to our ministry. Our club went from 35 to 45 students meeting at my house to about 200 students meeting in the school gym each week. We had exposure to more students, and parents felt better about dropping off their kids on campus, as opposed to some guy's house.

How to Get Kicked Off Campus

A big part of getting and maintaining access to your local campus is building trust with the school by *not* violating their rules. We told the administrators we wouldn't talk about God during school hours, and we kept our word. If a kid wanted to talk during school, and the opportunity arose to share Christ with him, I made an appointment to meet with him after school, usually over fast food. After school I had the freedom to share whatever I wanted with the kid. But I always respected the guidelines that the school outlined for us.

Maybe I don't have to tell you this, but a few youth pastors have made it difficult for the rest of us. When they deal with schools, they take an aggressive approach. They quote "God's law is above man's law," and once on campus, they talk about God anyway. And if these individuals aren't allowed on campus, then sometimes they can be found lurking around the campus at student events like "See You at the Pole," reminding the administration they "can't stop the power of the gospel" and handing out flyers for their youth group—against most schools' policies. These youth pastors' motives aren't all bad, but their methodology is very poor. And it's just disrespectful.

We need to keep the big picture in mind. Would it be better to be banned from campus and eliminate a huge open door to students? Or would it be better to have access to campus, build trust with students, and share with them off campus?

About a decade ago, I witnessed a great example of the type of catastrophe that the aggressive approach can have on local ministries. In this particular city, most of the schools at that time were open to having pastors on campus, as well as some on-campus programs. Many of the schools even allowed some campus ministry organizations to use the school's facilities after school hours for ministry programs where the gospel was preached. Things were good. Literally thousands of students were being reached through these on-campus contacts.

Then a well-known Christian organization brought in a speaker for a school assembly. The school trusted "the church" in this city, so it allowed the speaker to speak to the students, as long as he followed the rules of not talking about God during the assembly. The speaker agreed. In the middle of the assembly, the speaker had a change of heart and decided "God's law is above man's law." He boasted that nothing could stop him from sharing the Word of God. He blatantly preached the gospel to hundreds of students during this assembly. Parents flipped out, the school administration was outraged (and rightly so—the speaker didn't keep his commitment), and everything was shut down in the city. This particular school district didn't discriminate which organization did what. It just removed all ministries, pastors—you name it, they removed it from all campuses around the city. The open doors for reaching thousands of students a week were closed because one guy "felt led" to share the gospel with a few hundred students *one time*. Afterward, he simply said, "Blessed are those who are persecuted for their righteousness," and went on to his next location, leaving the city to clean up the mess he left in his wake.

We need to keep our commitments to our local schools. Not only is this biblical, but it's also smart!

Networking

You may have noticed that I keep mentioning some parachurch organizations. Because of my years with Youth for Christ, I can't help but encourage you to contact local campus ministry organizations in your area. Check if there are any Youth for Christ, Young Life, or Fellowship of Christian Athletes organizations (just to name a few) in your community. Meet with some of the youth workers from these organizations and find out what schools they have relationships with in the community. Hopefully they'll be open to introducing you to the administration or at least involving you in their ministry. Obviously, you might have to build trust with these campus ministries first. But these organizations can be a great help.

Student-Led Outreaches

In the United States, thanks to the equal access law, if there are any school clubs like the math club or chess club, then students may start a "Christian" campus club if they abide by the guidelines. Often these guidelines require a faculty person to oversee it and possibly open her classroom for meetings. They also require students to fill out the necessary paperwork to get the club approved by the administration.

Usually the above steps aren't difficult. The success or failure of student-led outreach clubs are really determined by the existence of two vital ingredients:

1. A group of godly, responsible, gregarious student leaders

2. A youth worker who is willing to equip and encourage these leaders on a weekly basis

If the above components exist, then the club can succeed.

However, most "Christian Clubs" are Bible clubs. And I'm not talking about the proverbial "Bible Club." I'm talking about an outreach club with a creative name and a purpose to reach out to unchurched kids.

Years ago I watched Jim, a friend and coworker, organize a student-led junior high campus outreach ministry that flourished. I was absolutely amazed. Initially I thought, "Junior high leaders? That's an oxymoron!"

I ate those words.

And I did so because Jim found a group of incredible junior high students with a passion for Jesus, as well as a willingness to work hard to reach their friends. That, combined with Jim's willingness to train and equip them, led to a successful ministry that reached a junior high campus better than most of the adult-led campus ministries I've seen.

After jumping through all the "hoops" of getting the club started, Jim equipped the students to program the club using the same method I've outlined in this chapter. The main difference was that Jim couldn't be there for the actual outreach. It was student-led and student-run. Jim would just meet with them after school the day before each club meeting and help them prepare.

Student-led clubs often have more open doors than adult-led clubs. They actually have the freedom to talk about God as much as they like. In the club Jim advised, they were even allowed to bring in guest speakers who "legally" could share about Christ within this student-led meeting. (Pretty cool, huh?) But the club stayed truly student-led with just a little after-hours help and guidance from my friend.

When preparing a student-led outreach club, both students and their adult advisors need to go through the steps I've outlined in this chapter.

WHEN

Another important option you need to consider is when to meet. This may be dictated by your location. For example, if the school gym is open to you, but only on Wednesday afternoons immediately after school, then that might have to be the time you meet! If it's a student-led club, you probably need to run it during lunch hour, like most other clubs.

But consider several elements when choosing the time, specifically with after-school outreach programs:

> • When are students available to come and hang out? It's nice to choose a time when students are already looking for something to do.
>
> • When are the sports activities that might compete for students' time? You don't want to lose all the football players because you run your program during practice.
>
> • When do sports practices end? This might be a great time to have it—immediately after practice.
>
> • Are there any large clubs or activities in the area that already draw out a large number of students? If so—when do they meet? You don't want to compete with these groups, either.

• Is there a local church that runs their youth group on a certain night? If we consider the future, you may not want to run your outreach at the same time because then you can't plug students into that youth group later. For years I ran outreach on a Wednesday and helped with a youth group on Thursday. I began inviting my outreach kids to youth group and many started attending both. The outreach program served as a stepping stone to the youth group.

You may not be able to comply with all of these, but they're all factors worth considering.

GETTING STARTED

Once you've decided when and where you're going to meet, you need to plan your weekly programming. At this point you've either gained access to the campus, or you've secured a meeting location somewhere near the school, one that's appealing to the students from that particular campus and available on a weekly basis.

So how do you get the students there?

You may already have momentum in place. In other words, there's something in existence already and you just have to build on it. In this case, you start spreading the word again and get ready to launch your weekly program. More on this later.

But some have nothing in place. Your heart is broken for lost students, and you want to do something about it. Maybe you even tried talking to the local campus, but they didn't allow you access.

Now what?

That's what happened to me years ago. When I went to work for Youth for Christ, my boss pointed me to a certain campus and said, "There. That's the one. We've been praying for a ministry on that campus for years."

I said, "Great. How many kids do we have involved?"

"None."

"How many volunteers?"

"None."

"Where will we meet?"

"You'll have to talk to the school and see."

I thought for a moment. "I guess I shouldn't ask what this job pays, huh?"

So there I was. No money, no help, no students, no location. It doesn't get much worse than that. So I started from scratch. I began doing what I described above—contacting the campus and trying to gain access to it. I asked if we could hold our Campus Life club on campus. Nope. I asked if I could come on campus at lunchtime and hang out with students. Nope. I asked if I could just help during yard duty for free. Nope. So it was definitely looking like I'd have to meet off campus.

I began recruiting friends of mine to help me with this crazy idea. I started talking with people I knew who were sold out for Christ and had a passion to reach out to others. I also put the word out that I wanted to meet some students from that school. I talked to anyone I knew who lived in the area and to my youth pastor friends around the city.

Within two weeks I met two teenagers. One was a kid from a local church who attended the school. The other was a girl who didn't go to church regularly, but happened to be visiting my friend's church one week.

I talked with both students—the "church kid" and "the girl"—and I shared what Campus Life was going to look like: Trips, events, and a fun weekly program. I invited them to a pizza place the next week, and I asked them to invite several of their friends to come along for free pizza so I could also tell them about this thing called "Campus Life."

This is an example of an important principle called "momentum." It's something that's rarely talked about in youth ministry programming, but it's absolutely essential. Some people try to start off a weekly program with a huge event—cold turkey. But this is risky if you don't build momentum first. "Momentum" basically means creating a stir or a buzz about your weekly program. It's spending several weeks—even months, if necessary—contacting students, getting them excited about this new weekly program, and building up expectations for all the fun that will be coming soon.

The next week I showed up at the pizza place with my wife and two potential volunteers. (I say "potential volunteers" because all I'd asked them to do was come have pizza with me and meet these students.) When we showed up, there were seven teenagers stuffed in a booth in the corner. The unchurched girl I'd already met had invited her brother and five other friends, and they were waiting for free pizza. I never saw the other boy I'd invited from the local church. I found out later that he never invited any of his friends, he just showed up at the pizza place about five minutes after I did. When he saw the group of "troublemakers" sitting in the booth with me, he turned right around and left.

The four of us sat in the booth with the seven students, ordered pizza, and began asking them questions.

"What's your favorite thing to do for fun during the week? What about on the weekends?"

Some students gave one-word answers. Others talked for five minutes at a time. And when they stopped, we asked them more questions.

"Have you ever gone camping? Have you ever gone water-skiing?"

Slowly the students began to open up more. They shared about their experiences, and then I said something about how we're planning several camping and waterskiing trips with Campus Life because Campus Life owned a water ski boat.

Then I asked them more questions: "Do you ever go snowboarding? Do you ever go play in the snow?"

More answers from the students. Then I mentioned, "Every year we have a weekend snow retreat with Campus Life."

We just listened to the kids for an hour. I asked questions about what they did for fun, what they liked about school, what they hated about school. What were their favorite movies and TV shows? What's the most recent CD they bought? What radio station did they listen to?

I threw in little tidbits about all the fun we'd have at Campus Life that year, but near the end I told them that it was going to be starting soon. "Every year we start with a big pizza bash where kids get all the pizza they can eat and all the Pepsi they can drink for $1." The students' faces lit up. I asked them, "How many friends do you think you could bring to that?" The teenagers now bragged about how many friends they could bring.

We finished by telling them the pizza bash would be coming up soon, so we wanted them to start bringing more friends. I gave them flyers for free root beer floats at my house the following week. Again, I was following the principles of building momentum. We told them about the pizza event, but we didn't jump into it too soon. I needed more students first. The free root beer floats were a way to draw more teenagers in the next week, but not put all my aces down yet.

The next week 12 students showed up at my house for root beer floats. I had each one fill out a "Campus Life Info." card, which collected their basic information (name, e-mail address, phone number, etc.).

Then I told them, "Before we get started with the root beer floats, I want to know if anyone here thinks they have good reflexes." Before they knew what was happening, I was leading them in a bunch of games. I never said, "Hey, let's play some games." I just asked them, "Who's hungry?" or "Who thinks they can shoot a marshmallow across the room and hit a two-inch target?" Those teenagers laughed and played games for 30 minutes. I had three adult volunteers helping me that night, and they played with the students, interacted with them, and got to know their names and a little bit about each of them. We all had a blast.

Then I gave what I call "the talk." It's an important element that allows me to be completely up-front with the students about my intentions. My goal with "the talk" is always two-fold:

> 1. I want to let students know we're a Christian organization, and we'll talk about who God is and how they can get to know him.
>
> 2. I don't want to scare them away.

When I worked with Campus Life, "the talk" sounded something like this:

> We're glad so many of you came out this week, and

we look forward to hanging out with you this year. At Campus Life we do a lot of fun things like tonight, as well as trips, retreats, crazy events, and camps. But Campus Life is more than just fun and games. We realize students are also looking for answers to tough questions. At Campus Life we'll have discussions about issues you're dealing with in your lives. We'll talk about friends, peer pressure, drugs and alcohol, gangs, and other topics relevant to what you're going through. Sometimes these topics will lead to discussions about God because we feel that's an important aspect of life. Every person on Campus Life staff is a Christian and cares about students and the decisions they're making daily. Don't worry, we're not going to try to get you to shave your heads and join a cult or something. We just want to provide a safe place where you can dialogue about some of the questions you have about life, and maybe get some of those questions answered. I think that you'll find that Campus Life is a great place to hang out and have fun. Speaking of fun—we're having our big pizza event in two weeks, and we want you to bring as many friends as possible. (*Share more about the event.*) But right now we're going to have some root beer floats!

Then we served root beer floats and handed out flyers for the next week. These flyers didn't have any "free food" as a draw; this would be our first time trying to draw them out with just the momentum of the experience we'd created. The flyer just said when, where, and had a map to the location. We invited them back for "more of the same" the next week at a gathering called "Campus Life." And 22 students showed up.

That week we played more games and we had a quick discussion on friendship. We played a game much like the newlywed game on the topic of friendship then asked some quick questions about friends—who they are and the qualities of a real friend. Some of these qualities were trust and faithfulness. I ended our time together with a question. I asked the students if they ever considered God as a friend, and then I read a verse about how God is faithful to us. For many of these students, it was the first time someone had cracked open a Bible in front of them. But I didn't go too far. I didn't give an altar call; I didn't turn up the heat and start preaching about hell. I just steered the discussion to God, then steered it back again before they got scared. I closed the discussion, and we just hung out for a while before I invited them back the next week.

The momentum built for a few more weeks, and we finally kicked off the year with almost 50 students in attendance at our pizza bash. I gave "the talk" again, and students came back the next week. Not 50 this time, but a bunch of them. We started averaging between 25 and 35 each week. Our discussions got deeper, too; we got to the point where we didn't shy away from gospel presentations.

But we always stayed true to our word. Campus Life continued to be about loving students and providing a safe place for them to have fun. Indeed, part of our love for them was sharing Christ with them, but that wasn't our only agenda. Teenagers see right through hidden agendas. And teenagers who didn't have any interest in God or the Bible were coming to our meetings. We loved them, too. I think some of them really benefited from all the discussions we had about life issues and all the speakers we brought in. Every one of those discussions segued to God and his love for us. Seeds were definitely planted in the lives of even the most resistant students.

PROGRAMMING IT WEEK AFTER WEEK...

Once momentum has begun, I program a campus outreach much like I would any weekly outreach program.

What does that look like?

I'm glad you asked. We'll devote the next chapter to that subject entirely.

planning weekly outreach programs

planning effective outreach programs week after week

More than 70 teenagers gather in the "high school center" of the church just off the highway. Candles are lit around the room and a coffee bar on the east end of the building is filled with students ordering lattés and mochas. Students are talking and laughing with each other as they hang out at the tables set up around the perimeter of the room. Adult volunteers mingle with students, greeting new students, calling the regulars by name.

Thirty minutes later the lights dim and everyone gathers on the floor as a band starts to play. The guy with the guitar welcomes everyone and introduces the music.

"Music is something we really like around here. We're going to sing a few songs and put the words on the screen. If you'd like to join us, please do. If not, feel free to just listen. We hope you enjoy the music. We worship God with this music...that's something else we really like to do around here."

Many of the Christian students sing along; some of the newcomers do, too. Others just listen and enjoy the comfortable atmosphere. After three songs a college kid goes up front and shares a story from his life—how he tried things "his way" and ended up flat on his face. Then he explains how a friend told him about Jesus and how that experience changed his life.

The band plays just two more songs and then the youth pastor gives a relevant talk about the pursuit of temporary things versus the pursuit of eternal things. Eighteen students stand up at the end of the night and give their lives to Christ.

How do you plan these kinds of programs?

Let's review for a few seconds. In the beginning of this book, we talked about general principles for planning outreach events. We defined an outreach event in chapter 2. In chapters 3 and 4 we talked about our purpose and our draw. In other words, *what we're trying to achieve and how we're going to get students there.* Chapter 5 told us how to start this process from scratch.

By the time you get to this chapter, I'm assuming you've already read those earlier chapters and taken those necessary steps. Because when you start a weekly outreach event, you need to do *all* the steps outlined in chapter 5 to begin the process. In addition, you'll use much of what you learned in chapter 6—programming the actual agenda.

But let's be honest, a weekly program is going to program a little differently than a huge youth rally. In some areas it's almost more difficult to come up with a continuous draw that will bring students out week after week.

So are there unique elements in weekly outreach programs?

Are they the same week after week?

What do these program agendas look like each week?

Let's take a peek.

UNIQUE WEEKLY OUTREACH ELEMENTS

A weekly outreach program is very similar to a big event. That means we need to take the same initial steps when we're planning weekly outreach programs that we do when we're planning big events.

Believe it or not, you'll need to invest just as much initial planning time into your weekly events. A large event might take 50 hours of planning, while starting a weekly outreach program might take a solid week or more of initial planning. But that's just in the beginning. Once it's up and running, the momentum will help carry it from week to week. Don't get me wrong; that doesn't mean the programming and publicizing is all done. But once the outreach is launched, it might only take you three to 10 hours weekly, depending on the size of the program.

Large events require a huge draw that can also require a huge budget. Likewise, weekly events may also require a huge draw initially. Hopefully, the students will eventually begin to think of your program as "the place to be" on Wednesday nights. You'll still need some kind of a draw, but it won't have to be as radical as the one you used in the beginning.

Large events require a huge number of volunteers. Weekly events also require volunteers, but a different type: A group of people willing to serve weekly, just loving teenagers and hanging out with them.

Programming weekly events is very similar to how we program a large event. We can use many of the concepts from chapter 6 in our weekly outreach programming, but let's be realistic. We don't have the resources week to week to book big-name bands and speakers. Weekly outreach programs are going to require some great programming that keeps students coming and reaches them with a relevant message each week.

So how do we get started?

STARTING A WEEKLY OUTREACH PROGRAM

As I stated above, we start the planning process the same way we begin planning any outreach program. Let's take another look at the five steps we outlined in chapter 5:

1. Pray: Give this program or event to God and bring him into the planning process at the beginning so it's his program, not your program.

2. Plan Your Purpose: Know the goal of your program or event. What end result are you shooting for? If this is an outreach program, then your goal will be to *reach out to those who don't know Jesus and point them toward him.* Everything you do with this program must help you achieve this goal.

3. Pinpoint Your Target Audience: Determine who you want to draw to this program. With outreach programs, remember you're drawing those who don't know Jesus, but also consider what age you'll target, what region, and maybe even more specifics.

4. Brainstorm Your Draw: What will bring your target students to this program or event? Your purpose isn't enough. You need to get them there.

5. Consider Your Resources: You need to consider your budget, your need for supplies and workers, and a plan for advertising. This step really helps you dive into the specifics of your program or event, evaluating what's feasible and what's just wishful thinking. It also provides you with rough budgets, supply lists, and worker lists.

Now let's consider what this process might look like with a weekly outreach event. We'll use the example of the church from the beginning of the chapter.

Prayer is still the first step. This doesn't mean quickly bowing your head and saying, "God, bless this food to the nourishment of our bodies...oh yeah...and this weekly outreach program that we're planning. Amen!" This step means discovering what God wants to do. How does God want to use *you* and your church to reach students who need Jesus?

Involve others in this process. If your church feels that God wants them to do something for non-Christian kids, then the whole church should be challenged to pray. Get the entire church to "own" the process with you. Get the pastor to pray with you. If the church is part of the process from the beginning, then they might respond better when they see teenagers wearing sagging pants to a church service. They'll have already prayed for those students.

Pray for direction as you plan. Read the Bible. Read the book of Acts. Read other books about reaching beyond your church walls and see how God speaks to you.

In the church example from the beginning of the chapter, that pastor shared a vision from the pulpit for reaching out to the community. He challenged the church to pray. They prayed, and the leaders not only felt God urging them to have a weekly outreach program, but they also felt God's leading to build a facility that would attract area teenagers. They began to envision a coffee bar and a room that could hold more than a hundred—a huge step for a small church.

Once God starts working on you (which you may be experiencing already—and that's why you're reading this book!), sit down and plan your purpose. (Refer back to chapter 3 where I outline how you need to write down the specific purpose of your program.) The aforementioned church decided that the purpose of their midweek program was to *point people to Jesus by sharing the gospel each week* and then following up with each new believer through one-on-one discipleship and plugging them into home Bible study groups.

They decided to target the high school students in their small town. The church was just down the street from Center High, so the location was perfect.

This church spent several months brainstorming their draw. The youth pastor decided *not* to survey the students. They'd done that before and found that teenagers didn't really know what they wanted. And many of the teenagers they asked were the wrong ones because the students they wanted to attract weren't attending church. So the youth pastor decided that observation was one of the better methods for deciphering what "drew" teenagers to programs, activities, or events.

The youth pastor and his volunteers began taking notes about where the high school students "hung out." The local Starbucks was a huge draw, as was a place in the school called "the student center." Both places offered comfortable seating, tables, food, and beverages—but mostly they offered a place to just hang out.

This is what sparked the idea for providing a place that was student-friendly and with the elements they seemed to enjoy. The idea for the coffee bar, dim lighting, and candles emerged. And it proved to be a huge success in this town.

This group took these ideas, evaluated the necessary resources, and made it happen. The whole church had been praying about doing something for the community, so when the request for donations was made from the pulpit, the whole church owned in. The pastor simply requested, "Pray and see what God lays on your heart to do." The church passed out response cards during the next several weeks, and this allowed people to pledge to contribute money or volunteer to serve in some way.

The youth pastor began recruiting volunteers from the church. He got them involved in a small way at first, serving coffee or helping with an event. These workers liked what they saw and they wanted to be more involved. Before long, a team of more than 15 workers started coming each week to the midweek outreach.

But the draw didn't stop at just a coffee bar. Students had to spread the word. The group kicked off the year with a concert event featuring a local band made up of some of the students in the community. Their first week featured the band and a five-minute talk from a college kid about "the quest for truth." They invited everyone back and passed out a "free coffee" certificate to everyone who came that week.

Even more students came the second week. Great coffee and a place to hang out—those two elements were all most teenagers needed to draw them in. But the programming didn't hurt, either. Each week there was hang-out time, fun music, relevant discussions, and time to interact with others.

How do we plan this kind of program agenda?

Planning a Weekly Outreach Agenda

Once we go through the five steps listed above, we need to program what the actual "agenda" will look like each week. This process is very similar to what we did in chapter 6, but not as cumbersome. Weekly programs will be unique in that they're usually much shorter than a large event. These programs probably won't have as many logistical requirements or require as much scrutiny during the planning process. But don't forget: We have to program them week after week.

As you can see, this can be both a blessing and a curse. It's difficult because we have to consistently come up with new stuff each week. This takes time, creativity, and resources. But it's also a good thing because once we find something that works, we can repeat the skeletal structure and just provide different "meat."

For example, we might plan a preprogram schedule with "hang out" time, food, and music for the first half hour. Then we may have a countdown five minutes before we kick off the actual program. We start with some crowd games, an upfront activity or skit, and then segue to a testimony, and finally a speaker.

If this format works, then teenagers actually get used to it and are more accepting of it. We won't have to reinvent the wheel each week; we just pencil in the specifics around our basic outline cast in pen.

This doesn't mean we don't break the monotony every once in a while. You can plan surprise elements within the "penned" skeletal structure, such as bringing in a special band or a guest speaker. Or you can just "toss" the whole structure every once in a while and do something totally different. This is where the Holy Spirit not only helps us in our planning but can also prompt us to detour from it one week. Discarding a program for one week won't usually cause us to break any commitments or veer from our purpose. For example, one week you might hand everyone a blanket, lead them outside under the stars, and invite them to sit down on the grass and talk about creation.

Weekly Programming Basics

So how do you plan a program that works?

Programs vary depending on the time you have to work with. Some youth workers might have very short time slots, especially those doing on-campus outreaches (like we discussed in chapter 7) where you might only have 20 to 30 minutes to do your program.

In his *Dynamic Communicators Workshop*, Ken Davis says, "If you can't say it in five minutes, it's not worth being said." I think the same is true in youth ministry programming. I believe that if you can learn to program a 20-minute youth program, you can program most anything!

How can you draw students in, open a discussion, and wrap it up effectively in an allotted amount of time? That's what a youth worker named Daryl asked me in a recent e-mail to our youth ministry Web site:

Jonathan,

I am a YFC worker in Canada and have been so for many years. Recent changes in our school systems caused a much shorter lunch period than we have been accustomed to. Now, by the time the teens come and go, we have about 20 min. max to open, discuss, and close a topic. We need some ideas on how to develop a short meeting system that is interesting and efficient. Any ideas? Thanks.

—Daryl, Canada

Great question—and one that those of us who typically plan 90-minute programs should also pay attention to. How do we prepare an effective 20-minute program?

This is important because if we can learn to program something in 20 minutes, those basic principles transcend to the 60-, 90- and 120-minute programs as well. (I almost prefer the shorter times—especially with junior highers!)

1. BEGIN WITH THE END. Start with your purpose or end result in mind. Then program backward from there. If your purpose is to share the gospel, then your first goal is to perfect a different three-to-five-minute gospel presentation each week. I say three to five minutes because I'm keeping in mind that we only have a total of 20 minutes. And, considering the fact that we'll probably have at least four "stages" in our program, that gives us a maximum of five minutes for each "stage."

Remember, we're planning backward—starting at the end. So now that I've allocated a three-to-five-minute slot for my gospel presentation at the end, I need to ask myself, "How will we get there?" In other words, "What's going to provoke that gospel presentation?"

Most of the time you're not going to stand up in front of the room and say, "You need Jesus! Now shut up and listen to how you can be washed by the blood!"

2. OPENING THE DOOR TO THE GOSPEL. We need to provide relevant talks or discussions that meet teenagers where they are and deal with the issues they're dealing with every day. Remember, every student who sits through our program is probably asking, "Why should I be sitting here instead of at home browsing MySpace.com right now?" We need to provide real and relevant things to make them want to stay and listen.

Some leaders might use topical discussions to talk about the issues teenagers are going through. You might talk about sex one week or the topic of relationships. You might talk about loneliness or death.

Other youth workers like to develop their own talks and discussions. Still others will purchase curriculum or books with ready-made creative talks and discussions.

In our ministry we realize there's a weekly need for this kind of material. So each week at www.TheSourceForYouthMinistry.com

we try to plan new discussion starters, openers, talks, lessons, and video clip ideas for you to use in your min. These pages have discussion starters that jump-start discuss and segue into a wrap-up or gospel presentation. Many ɔ these pages also have small-group discussion questions you can use if your program lasts longer than just 20 minutes. Twenty minutes leaves no time for small groups.

3. WHAT IS YOUR WEEKLY DRAW? Now, continuing to work backward, we need a fun activity that will draw students to come. Hopefully we've already spent considerable time on this, but let's talk about it more specifically and in terms of our weekly outreach. Because it's a weekly outreach program, we need to create a continual draw week in and week out.

In the case of a campus lunch program, like the one mentioned earlier, we need to ask, "What will bring students to our program during lunch?" My guess is that if we just put up flyers that say "Come to Campus Life where we'll tell you about Jesus," chances are numbers will be small. So how can we draw students in so we create opportunities to share Christ with them?

So often, especially in the church, we forget this step. We don't put much time into the draw. We just hope students will come to our Wednesday night programs because, after all, we've always had a program on Wednesday night. Then we encourage teenagers to bring their friends when we really haven't considered what it is that we're asking students to invite their friends to. Are we providing something fun and relevant that our students can invite their friends to? Many unchurched students will attend an outreach program if they're invited by friends.

We don't have to run *Fear Factor* games every week. Fun activities can be a draw, but so can "relevant" teaching and discussions. Most of the unchurched kids at the school around the corner are looking for something. They're looking for an answer to the emptiness in their lives. We've got that answer, and relevant teaching is magnetic. I've seen numerous ministries draw students because of their creative discussions or relevant teaching alone.

In our last chapter we talked about an important principle that is often ignored in youth ministry programming—building momentum. With our weekly outreach programs, we must realize that the first few weeks of programming are very important and first impressions are key. If we can build momentum with fun activities and relevant discussions in our program, thereby drawing students back each week, they'll begin to trust our program. They'll return simply because it's now "the place to be." (If you haven't read the previous chapter, make sure you do. It gives a great example that outlines how we can build momentum with our weekly program.)

That doesn't mean we don't have to continue to create fun and relevant programming each week. After all, each week brings new students, which means we're building new momentum. But we do need to realize the importance of the first few weeks.

With campus clubs, during the first few weeks we might want to use some of these ideas for our draw during lunchtime:

- Inflatables, like jousting arenas or boxing rings

- Napoleon Dynamite dance contest

- Root beer floats

- Free pizza

The sky's the limit. And don't forget to mix things up throughout the year by offering special events like this every once in a while.

Putting It All Together in a Program

Each week we should have something fun that draws students in and gets their attention. With junior high students, crazy games work. A general principle that I used to use is this: *Start with something everyone can do, then do something that entertains the group from up front* (that way you begin to focus the attention up front).

So you might start with an activity like the "I Need a Shoelace" game from our www.TheSourceForYouthMinistry. com's Audience Games page. Then do the "Happy Shake" game from our Sick and Twisted Games page.

Now our 20-minute program's basic layout might look like this:

- Fun opening activity that draws students/gathers attention (5 minutes)

- Up-front game or activity that focuses the students' attention up front (4 minutes)

- Opener—discussion starter/video clip that starts a discussion on the topic (3-5 minutes)

- Gospel presentation (3-5 minutes)

This is just a 20-minute program example. Obviously, if you have more time, you can add more hang-out time, skits, creative announcements, some small group time, or even more time for full-length curriculum or talks. Then, using the techniques and principles we learned in chapter 6, you can fine-tune your agenda with solid transitions and some fun elements to make the program flow smoothly.

planning weekly outreach programs

If you can learn to effectively program just 20 minutes—you can program most anything.

A Normal Part of Weekly Programming

Weekly outreach programs are incredible tools for reaching a community. More churches are beginning to include a weekly outreach program as a normal part of their weekly programming.

I've visited churches that have their outreach program on Tuesday nights and their growth and discipleship program on Thursday nights. I've seen some churches offer a midweek outreach program one night and then offer small groups in people's homes as their growth and discipleship programming on other days of the week.

The church I attend right now is pastored by a guy who says our church is for "people who don't like church." The church's leadership team really makes an effort to bring out unchurched people each Sunday. Consequently, we have a ton of unchurched kids visiting on Sunday mornings. So our junior high pastor is using this opportunity to run his outreach program on Sunday morning at 11 AM. (He claims that if he did it any earlier, students wouldn't show up.) He tells his regular attendees to bring friends on Sunday mornings. The program is fun and evangelistic. Several hundred students show up each Sunday.

Weekly outreach events can have many different faces, but diverse methods reach a diverse group of people.

Just keep giving them something to bring their friends to!

programming large events
reaching out with a larger scope—citywide events

Driving on Interstate 10 between Los Angeles and Phoenix, I was heading toward a speaking engagement when I received the phone call.

"We want to do a citywide event. We hope to bring out people from 30 area churches."

I loved her passion. She was a part-time youth worker from a small church just outside Omaha, Nebraska. She had anywhere from 15 to 20 students in her youth group each week, but she had a vision for something much bigger.

"We want you to come and speak, but we don't have any idea what we're doing. We've never done this before."

It wasn't the first time I'd heard this. Our ministry's Web site often connects me with youth workers with a vision for a large event like this, but little resources or experience to pull it off. I talked with this youth worker from Palm Springs to the Arizona border. Her church had been praying about doing something to reach the community. They just didn't know exactly what it would look like.

I asked if she'd shared her vision with any other youth workers. She had. In fact, she was meeting with five other youth workers from other small churches within 10 miles of her church. They'd been praying about reaching their community and communicating with their senior pastors about their vision for a citywide event. Each of the churches had already opted in with a commitment of $250 to $500 each.

This youth worker didn't know it, but before she ever called me she was already becoming an expert on how to launch a citywide event. She'd been laying the groundwork that is crucial with this type of event.

In a way, launching a citywide event isn't much different than planning any other type of outreach program or event. We still need to go through the planning and programming steps we learned in chapters 5 and 6:

1. Pray: Give this program or event to God and bring him into the planning process at the beginning so it's his program, not your program.

2. Plan Your Purpose: Know the goal of your program or event. What end result are you shooting for? If this is an outreach program, then your goal will be to *reach out to those who don't know Jesus and point them toward him*. Everything you do with this program must help you achieve this goal.

3. Pinpoint Your Target Audience: Determine who you want to draw to this program. With outreach programs, remember you're drawing those who don't know Jesus, but also consider what age you'll target, what region, and maybe even more specifics.

4. Brainstorm Your Draw: What will bring your target students to this program or event? Your purpose isn't enough. You need to get them there.

5. Consider Your Resources: You need to consider your budget, your need for supplies and workers, and a plan for advertising. This step really helps you dive into the specifics of your program or event, evaluating what's feasible and what's just wishful thinking. It also provides you with rough budgets, supply lists, and worker lists.

6. Plan Your Program Agenda: Actually plan out "what happens when." This is where you put all your planning into a precise format that's going to be the most effective for achieving your purpose.

This is the same process we'd go through with a citywide event—with one exception. A citywide event demands networking and partnership with others in the community.

How can we do this?

THE COMMITTEE/WORK TEAM

Several years ago I wanted to do an event in our city to talk to teenagers about sex, drugs, and music. (Yes, sex, drugs, and rock 'n' roll, but I didn't call it that.) Like many of you longtime youth workers, for the last decade I'd noticed teenagers making progressively worse choices in these areas of their lives, and I felt teenagers weren't equipped to make better choices. So I set out to launch an event that would help them do that.

That was the beginning of my vision for an event called "Tough Choices."

I had the broken heart, I had the title, and I had the vision. But that was all I had.

Ever been there?

So I started with step one in the process—prayer. As I prayed, I started sharing my vision with some friends and asked them to pray, too. Pretty soon a few of us were praying. We prayed for God to guide our vision. We prayed for the budget. We prayed for area youth leaders and that God would help us meet a need in our community. Then we all started sharing the vision with others.

Finally, I decided to form a committee.

I know, some people think *committee* is a bad word. My father, who teaches management in the corporate world, told me the proper term is "work team." You can call it a work team, a committee, a task force—whatever has positive connotations in your community. I chose the word *committee* because in my area, youth workers didn't want another thing on their plate, and the words *work* or *task* might have scared them off.

I had a good friend and pastor who used to say, "If you ever want to take 10 times as long to do something, join a committee!" And I understand his frustration. I've been in some of those kinds of committees—just a bunch of red tape. But I'm not talking about that kind of committee. I'm talking about gathering a team of people to help build the momentum and carry out the vision for your event.

I called up nine of my friends; a few of them were also coworkers. I called up three youth pastors from large churches nearby. I also called three youth pastors from small churches in the area. Then I invited a leader from a local campus ministry, the leader of a local "Teen Moms" program, and a local business guy who had a heart for teenagers. Most of these people had already heard the buzz about this vision; some had already been praying with me.

I invited them all to Denny's for a free breakfast. I chose breakfast because a couple of the youth workers from the smaller churches also had full-time jobs. All but one of these nine people showed up.

Whenever we plan a large event or a citywide event, it's always good to bring others into the process during the beginning stages. I'll actually start some of the basic planning for the event before I form the committee, but I always have a committee formed before I get to step five.

My old boss at Youth for Christ planned numerous citywide events over the last two decades, and he's a great example of how to do this process. He often petitioned others to pray with him for a certain vision he had to reach the community. He and a few others would usually plan a purpose, pinpoint a target audience, and figure out a draw. But before he went any further than that, he'd gather together a team of people and share his vision. The team always appreciated that he'd already taken planning steps. He wasn't coming to them with a blank piece of paper.

That's what I did at Denny's that morning. I shared my heart for students. Then I shared my vision for "Tough Choices." I told them what I thought the event would look like, who I wanted to bring out to this event, and how we'd draw students out. Then I announced that I wanted each of them to join me in bringing this event to the city.

We brainstormed some details and expanded the vision, but I basically left them all with a challenge to pray and see if God was leading them to be a part of this event. I asked them all to tell me within the month.

Because of the relationships we'd already built in that community, all but one person joined the team.

Planning as a Committee/Work Team

At our next meeting (back at Denny's again), we started where I'd left off, step five: Considering our resources.

We talked about the best location for the event. One of the guys from a big church volunteered his church building for the location. Everyone agreed it was a fantastic location, if he could reserve it. Right there at the table, he called the church secretary from his cell phone and reserved the building for us (more than six months out).

We talked about the speakers we wanted. I had a friend—a great speaker—who owed me a favor and was going to give us a deal. The committee liked the idea. We talked about other possible speakers and assigned that task to be completed quickly. The availability of desirable speakers wasn't guaranteed. We needed to nail those details quickly.

With big events, some of the first details you'll have to nail down are the date, location, bands or entertainment, and speakers. And all of those items have to line up on the same calendar. Believe me, it's quite a relief once those big items are written in ink.

At our next breakfast, we were happy to have the big items penned in. We planned even more of the fine details and even started on step six: Planning our program agenda. We decided to use two teen emcees. Two members of the group had the perfect candidates for the job. These students met with me to "audition" for the part a week later and, sure enough, they were ideal.

As for marketing our event, one of the committee members knew an executive from the local Christian radio station. They generously donated air time to us, interviewed us on one of the talk shows, and gave away tickets to the event several weeks before the event.

The program started coming together perfectly. Ideas from around the table helped us plan out resources or solutions for almost every possible outcome.

The day of the event finally arrived. We hoped for 1,000 in attendance. As it turned out, we had just over 1,000—880 students and the rest were pastors, youth workers, and adult volunteers. Not bad for our first year. God really blessed the event.

But it wouldn't have been half of what it eventually turned out to be if I'd tried to take it on alone.

Who Do You Want on Your Committee?

When I select who I want on my committee, I look for key youth leaders in my community from churches large and small. In this search, I always make sure I choose the four W's: Wisdom, weight, wealth, and worker.

- **Wisdom:** I want people who will help us make wise choices. Some wisdom comes with experience, some with age. I look for both. I want people who've been down some of these roads before. I want people who understand the large church and people who understand the small church.

- **Weight:** I also want people of influence. Their very presence helps endorse the project. I want that one person who knows "everybody" in the city.

- **Wealth:** I want people with resources. They might not be able to fund it themselves, but they know the people who will.

- **Worker:** Some people are just born workers. They don't have to be asked to get things done. They might not know anyone, but they'll work harder than the other eight people combined.

The more people you bring along with you, the more momentum you can start building. With our "Tough Choices" event, there were six of us on the committee who had youth groups and were committed to bringing them to the event. So we had more than 200 students almost guaranteed, just from the youth workers sitting around the table at Denny's.

But it didn't stop there. Each team member committed to personally invite at least five other youth groups to the event. I literally whipped out a pad of paper during the third meeting and asked, "Dave, which five youth leaders are you inviting?" Dave listed his five. "Roger?" His five. All around the table, we each listed five. Sure, all of these churches didn't respond, but they were all personally invited by one of these youth workers and encouraged to come.

The Test of Time

In the last several years I've observed that many of these citywide events "earn trust" over time.

I've sat in hundreds of youth network meetings where a youth pastor stands up, holds up a poster, and announces that his church is doing a huge citywide event and would like to invite us all to bring our youth groups—next Friday.

Rarely do any more than just one or two other youth groups show up to these "spontaneous" events. Why? First, we weren't involved in the process from the beginning. And second, we've seen 20 of these events offered by one church or another in the last couple of years. They all claim this is just the first year and it will become an annual event, but it doesn't turn out the way they expected, so it only happens one year.

It's sad, but most youth workers are skeptical of the events they're invited to. Let's face it: Either we don't know the people planning it or it's not our denomination. But the bigger issue for most youth workers is that we don't want to go to an event unless we trust it.

It's like when we hear about a new film, we ask, "Who's in it?"

"No one big."

That's not very convincing. "No thanks."

If we don't recognize anyone, we usually skip it.

In bigger cities, the same can be true for events. In some cities, youth events are a dime a dozen. In my city there are about 15 different "big events" just in September. It's like a buffet of events.

Guess which events people always attend?

The ones they trust.

In a small town this is true also. Sure, there aren't 15 events offered in September alone. There probably haven't been 15 events in the last 15 years! But you've still seen the phenomenon. Someone launches a huge event. If it's successful the first year, the word spreads. Students start talking about it.

"Were you at the big event at that little white church in Macarthur last Friday night?"

"No. But I heard two girls talking about it at lunch. Is it true about that *Texas Chainsaw Massacre* hay ride?"

"It was the scariest thing I've ever been on!"

Next year the word spreads further and even more students show up. Each year the event gets bigger and bigger, building momentum from year to year. People come back because they "trust" the event. They didn't the first year because they'd never heard of it. But now the event has a reputation.

When I worked for Youth for Christ in Sacramento, we started an event called "First Fridays." It was a citywide event on the first Friday of every month. We mailed invitations to 900 churches in the greater Sacramento area, and we were in regular contact with about 70 or 80 of them. Depending on the month, we'd have between 200 and 300 students show up.

We tired quickly. It was difficult to program effectively for a monthly event. We quickly changed it to every other month. That soon changed to once a quarter. After a couple years, the momentum finally started to grow. We changed the name to "XtremZ" and marketed it as just four spectacular events a year.

Then those events grew in size, and we eventually dropped two of them and started concentrating on doing just two a year, but doing them very well.

By this time, hundreds of churches had been to our events. Attendance continued to grow, and more growth meant a bigger budget. A bigger budget allowed more activities, and more activities meant bigger draw. The event just kept growing. We'd earned their trust.

I remember a small-town youth worker who was discouraged when only 300 students showed up to a citywide event. I didn't understand why she was upset. This was a small farm town in Iowa with one high school. I told her 300 students is a great turnout for a first-year event in a town that size.

Not only that, but also everyone leaving the event was talking about how great it was. And I heard some of the planning team members talking about all of the groups who couldn't make it to the event. Guess what? They'll make it next year because everyone in town was talking about that event the next Sunday at church, the next Monday morning at their junior high school and high school. Even workplaces were buzzing about the "town youth rally" last weekend. The event had not only been successful, but it had already begun to earn trust in people's minds.

THE GATEKEEPERS

In chapter 4 we detailed how to draw students. With many outreach programs and events, we can market directly to students. But with citywide events, that's not always the case. The "gatekeeper" is the person on whom we need to focus 80 percent of our marketing efforts. And youth workers are often the biggest gatekeepers. After all, it's the youth worker, pastor, or volunteer in charge of the youth ministry who decides where the youth will be going on a Friday night in July. This person has the power to encourage their church kids to invite their unchurched friends to the event. So if we can sell the gatekeeper on our event, then he'll bring eight students, 30 students, or 200 students, depending on the size of his group.

Some gatekeepers have their own gatekeepers. In my city we learned that in certain churches, the senior pastor was the gatekeeper to the youth pastor. In other churches, the secretary was the gatekeeper. Some youth pastors never received any of our mailings because the secretary tossed them all before he ever saw them.

Regardless, we need to find the gatekeepers.

Remember what I said in chapter 4 about speakers *not* being a draw? Well, that's *not* the case at all with citywide events. At citywide events our gatekeepers are the big decision makers. Sure, a typical outreach kid has no idea who Reggie Dabbs or Louie Giglio is and they probably don't care to know. But youth workers care. Pastors care. Many of them may have heard a speaker at the last youth convention or at least heard of her through the youth network. And believe me, certain speakers carry "trust." A good speaker can be an additional draw to a gatekeeper—not *the* draw, but a draw.

Nevertheless, we must remember the focus of our event. If our focus is outreach, then we need to be careful about how we market the event to church youth groups. The tendency for a church youth group is to bring all their church kids. After all, church kids need events too. But we don't want to just bring out believers. I'm not saying all church attendees are believers. We all know that a lot of church attendees still need Christ. But in any case, we also want to target those students who aren't going to church. It's vital to spread the word that this is the perfect event to bring friends to. We don't want churches to just bring their seven committed students. We want those seven students to pray about this event for months and each invite three friends to the event. Create incentives for the group that brings the most friends.

This kind of marketing and publicity is done through the gatekeeper. So don't underestimate the importance of communication with the gatekeepers.

You probably noticed in my Tough Choices event example that I really emphasized the importance of inviting other youth workers. Each committee member was responsible for contacting five churches. With eight of us on the committee, that meant we were going to visit and personally invite 40 churches to the event.

Personal contact with gatekeepers is vital. Flyers and invitations are a dime a dozen, but a call from a friend and a personal invitation speaks volumes. Then committee members can keep the communication channels open throughout the publicity of the event. Each committee member can present the event to their five groups and challenge them to bring friends.

This brings up the subject of networking. Cities that already have a youth network in existence have a 100 percent easier time making an event like this happen. For some of us, that means the first step we should take in any event planning is starting to build relationships with area youth workers. As these relationships develop, maybe you can eventually start up a quarterly youth network meeting where youth pastors get together and encourage each other and learn from each other.

Web sites like the National Network of Youth Ministries (NNYM) site (www.YouthWorkers.net) can be a great resource to help youth workers come together.

HE CHOSE TO USE US

It doesn't matter if you live in a big city or a small town. A large citywide event is possible in your community. It takes time, prayer, planning, and a group of people who will own the process together. God wants to reach our communities. He could do it by himself, but he chose to use us to do it.

If you're feeling God tugging at your heart to do something—don't stifle it. Start with step one. Pray, and see what God has in mind for your community.

sidestepping speakers who just don't "get it"...

...and booking speakers who do

The event was perfect. More than 1,000 students had shown up. The activities during the night were a success. The logistics had flowed flawlessly so far, and most importantly, students were having a blast. Six months of planning were about to come to a close. Only 40 minutes left to go—just the speaker and the altar call. What could go wrong?

The emcee introduced the speaker.

The speaker started his tantrum. No one remembers his exact words, but he did a lot of pointing. He also kept yelling, "What are you thinking?"

Students just glanced at each other at first. "Is he serious?" "Is this a joke?"

The speaker continued to yell, "Everyone stand up!" He walked down to the audience, selected a boy wearing a brown Abercrombie sweater in the front row, and barked at him, "Do you know what would happen to you if you died tonight and stood before the gates of heaven?!"

The speaker shoved the mic in front of the terrified teenager's face as silence fell over the crowd. The kid froze.

Meanwhile, the jaws of eight planning committee members hit the floor.

The speaker moved to his next victim, a skinny blonde wearing low-cut jeans and a tank top. He shoved the microphone in her face. "How about you?"

She looked to her friend for help.

Nothing.

"I guess I'd..." she paused. "I don't know."

The speaker yanked the mic back. "She says, 'I don't know'!"

I wish I could tell you I'm just making this story up, but this really happened during an event in my city last year.

Most of us have been to an event or program that had bad speakers. Maybe not as inappropriate and irresponsible as this guy, but we've all experienced speakers who just didn't cut it.

I assure you—plenty of bad speakers are out there. Most of them don't mean to be bad, but they are. For some, it's their lack of speaking ability. Apparently, they've never evaluated their spiritual gifts. They think their gift is teaching, but it's really not. They're like those people on the first week of *American Idol* who claim, "Everyone says I'm the best singer they've ever heard!" They sound very convincing—until they start singing.

For other bad speakers, it has nothing to do with ability or talent; it has everything to do with discernment. I've listened to many talented speakers who made choices onstage that everyone in the room regretted. Onstage and in front of a bunch of teenagers is a bad place to make a big mistake.

I believe we can learn some valuable lessons from bad speakers, so I'm going to describe a few different types that I've run into time and time again.

SPEAKERS TO AVOID

Let Me Hear You Say "Jesus!"

Years ago I programmed a special concert event for our weekly on-campus ministry. We had a few hundred teenagers show up on this particular Wednesday night, and we were excited about the attendance and the fact that the event was going as planned.

Our entertainment was a Christian rapper who was going to rap and dance. Teenagers loved his music—my draw. He was also going to share his testimony with the students—my purpose: Sharing the gospel. I'd heard him speak before, and he always did a great job.

Unfortunately, I didn't know he was bringing a buddy with him, and his buddy couldn't wait to get that microphone in his hand.

I'd spent hours talking with the rapper about our event and our audience. He understood our purpose, and he had a good grasp of who was going to be there that night. Almost all of these students didn't go to church. They were just normal, secular school students coming out for a rap concert. Unfortunately, "Buddy" wasn't in these meetings with us, and the rapper never communicated this information to his friend.

As "Buddy" took the stage, his first words were in the form of a chant. I'll never forget it because it was pretty unique. He just kept saying the name "Jesus." Nothing else—just "Jesus."

"Jesus, Jesus, Jesus, Jesus, Jesus, Jesus…" and then he closed his eyes and had a little prayer moment. The students just stared at him. Then he opened his eyes and went on. He yelled, "Let me hear you say Jesus!" and then he held his mic out for the audience to shout back. A handful of students started to yell, but they only got as far as "Jes—" when they realized they were alone. Laughter began trickling through the crowd.

The situation was obvious. This guy was used to doing "Christian" concerts. He'd never been in front of a secular crowd before, and it was obvious. Afterward "Buddy" commented, "Wow, what's wrong with these kids?"

I'd worked with these students for a year. I knew exactly what was "wrong with these kids." They needed Jesus, but they certainly weren't going to listen to anyone who made them chant his name.

We have the awesome opportunity to share Christ with a generation who needs him desperately. In the beginning of this book, I shared an interesting truth when it comes to programming outreach events: *Remember your audience. They don't know Jesus, so don't treat them like they do!* We need to use speakers who understand their audiences.

Ssssh! Don't Say *Jesus*

I had just the *opposite* problem a few years ago. I booked a speaker from a church that claimed to be a "seeker" church. I brought him to my group, and I asked him to share the gospel with them. We talked about the students and the purpose of my event, and he seemed to have a good understanding. He claimed he really understood the kinds of students I was reaching out to.

I was excited. After all, most speakers I'd encountered had the opposite problem; they didn't understand non-Christian kids at all. Maybe that's why I didn't see what was coming.

His speech was very good. It would've been a great talk for a high school assembly. He had the students laughing, and he kept their attention. There was just one problem: He never presented the gospel. This guy never even said the word *Jesus* or *God*. He was like a public service announcement or a "say no to drugs" commercial.

At the end I asked him what happened. He didn't have a clue.

I thought for a moment, and then I asked him if he'd heard me when I asked him to present the gospel.

He said, "Oh, I thought you just meant 'the truth.'"

After that we got into a big discussion about how to share Jesus with outreach kids. He was pretty sure the best way to do it was not to mention the word *Jesus*.

I'm still scratching my head over that one.

Let me be very clear. If you're doing a program at a school or someplace where you've agreed *not* to share about Jesus, then *don't*. And if you're doing an event where the purpose is to point to Jesus through an act of service, then your actions will speak for themselves. And if you're doing an event where your purpose is simply to invite students back to church or the youth group, then that's okay, too.

But if you're doing a program where you *are* allowed to share about Jesus and that's the *purpose* of your event, then please—DO SHARE JESUS.

Remember your purpose. It's to point people to Jesus. Don't forget to do that.

Clock? What Clock?

This speaker doesn't know there's an invention called "the clock."

Yes, I'm very organized. Okay, I'm meticulous. But when I tell speakers they can talk for 30 minutes and they say, "Okay, that's fine," then I guess I'm just "meticulous" enough to believe them. That's why I was shocked to hear one speaker still flapping his big yapper 56 minutes after he'd started talking to my students.

It's not that he was boring. He was actually very good. But I had parents showing up, and they wanted to know what was going on. Two janitors at the school we'd rented were threatening to turn off the power.

I waited until the guy took a dramatic pause, and then I grabbed the microphone and quickly said, "Let's hear it for—!" (Not a bad transition. I don't think too many students noticed he wasn't really finished.) In any case, the event was now over. So much for the invitation.

That night I had more than 20 counselors trained and waiting with counseling materials in hand. Now I had to apologize and thank each of them for coming out anyway. Needless to say, not many of them came the next time I called.

I asked the guy what happened. He told me "the Spirit led him" to keep talking.

The next day I was sitting in the vice-principal's office apologizing and promising to make amends with two irate janitors. (It was my first time being called into the principal's office since high school!)

Speakers need to keep within the time allotted. Sometimes they don't seem to understand that there are logistical consequences if they talk too long.

sidestepping speakers who just don't "get it" ...

Everybody's Invited

The speaker was highly recommended. He toured with a big-name ministry, and he'd been speaking for years. That's why I didn't hesitate to use him for our event.

But I guess I forgot to clarify our goal for the event: To reach out to unchurched kids and share the gospel with them. Since unchurched kids were our target audience, our focus was on first-time decisions. We wanted to present the gospel clearly and provide an opportunity for students to commit their lives to Christ. We *didn't* want to have a pep rally. There's a big difference.

Let's say our audience is 50 percent believers and 50 percent unbelievers. What if we present the gospel, but then say, "Anyone who chooses to follow Christ—please stand up"? Who's supposed to stand? Shouldn't our committed leadership kids stand up? Aren't they ready to follow Christ?

That's what happened at this event. The speaker did a pretty good job of getting the students' attention and keeping it for his entire talk. But at the end, he didn't really give an altar call. Instead, he just said, "Everyone who's ready to take a stand for Jesus—stand up!"

More than half the audience stood up.

More than 1,000 people had come to this event, and we had about 100 counselors ready to talk with kids one-on-one, or even one-on-two. After all, 200 responses would have been great. But imagine the look on our counselors' faces when nearly 700 students stood up. Then the speaker led them out the door to the counselors. Absolute chaos.

Our invitations shouldn't be so vague at outreach events.

I hate to say this, but this can be a pride issue with some speakers. They don't like to give an invitation and receive no response. And let's face it—it looks even better if hundreds of people stand up to make a decision.

I've heard speakers try to give an invitation where they tell a really sad story, getting everyone all emotional. Then, when everyone's crying, they ask, "If you feel something inside right now...that's probably God telling you to get up. Just come up right now and get saved."

I've counseled at some of these events. The first question a counselor should always ask is, "Why did you come forward tonight?" The answer I tend to get after this type of altar call is, "I don't know. I was just so sad!"

Sure, in this counseling situation I'll still present the gospel to people one-on-one and ask if they're ready to make that decision. But many of them aren't. They just thought the story about the guy's German shepherd that died was really sad.

Whenever I'm giving an invitation at an outreach event, I try to be clear and present the gospel as it is. I don't water it down one bit. I don't want to give anyone the idea that all they have to do is walk forward and say a couple words to be saved. That's just not biblical.

I present a clear message of what the Bible says. It doesn't matter what passage I'm using, they all require the same thing: We need to realize we can't do it our own way, and we need to give God control. Whether we're talking about "repenting" (stop going your own way, do a 180-degree turn, and go God's way, like in Acts 3:19, "Repent, then, and turn to God, so that your sins may be wiped out, that times of refreshing may come from the Lord") or we're talking about "belief" (like in Romans 10:9, "That if you confess with your mouth, 'Jesus is Lord,' and believe in your heart that God raised him from the dead, you will be saved"), the gospel message needs to be clear.

After I've clearly presented the biblical gospel message and I'm ready to invite people up, I might ask them like this:

If you're tired of grabbing onto the temporary thrills of life...if you're tired of trying to collect all kinds of nice stuff, only to live on a shaky foundation...then why not ask Jesus to take over? Why don't we let go of all these temporary thrills and put our faith in Jesus? Step up onto a firm foundation—a relationship with Jesus Christ. Let go of the old temporary stuff and grab onto a relationship with him.

It might not be easy. After all, some of us really want to hold onto that old stuff of ours. But let's face it—that old stuff hasn't really filled our emptiness. And you can't grab onto Christ if you're still holding onto something else.

If you're tired of holding onto the temporary and you'd like to let go of it and grab onto a relationship with Christ, there's no better time to do that than tonight. Tonight you can make that commitment. It's not just a decision; it's a commitment. It's saying, "Enough of the old, I'm ready to put my trust in Jesus."

If you've never made this commitment before, then I encourage you to do it now. If you're really ready to take that step of faith, pray with me now.

Then I end by praying and asking people to raise their hands, or, if I have counselors available, I invite students to come forward so we can pray with them and give them a gift (usually a new Bible).

If you think the above example doesn't leave room for rededications, sometimes I add something like the following:

Maybe you've made this decision before; but for

some reason, you never really gave control over to Jesus. You've been trying to hold onto your old stuff and Jesus at the same time. Guess what? It's not working. Maybe tonight you need to take the step of faith and let go of whatever it is you're holding onto and grab onto what Christ is offering.

We need to be about spreading the gospel, not spreading a false sense of security. So make sure your gospel presentations are biblical, not watered down—even if that means fewer students will come forward. And if your focus is outreach, make sure your invitations are specifically inviting people to make a new commitment to Christ. We shouldn't turn an altar call into a Christian pep rally.

The Sleeping Pill

I don't remember his name, and I don't remember a word that came out of his mouth. I just remember it was the longest 30 minutes of my life!

I'd brought 30 students to the event. Only a couple of them went to church; the rest needed Christ desperately. I was excited about this outreach event because this would be the first time many of these students would hear the gospel.

The activities at the event were fun. My students even liked the band—which wasn't always the case. Everything was going well—until the speaker was introduced.

I don't think his theology was bad. I don't think his motives were bad. The guy was just straight-up boring! And my students hated me for making them listen to him.

"Come on! How long do we have to listen to this guy?"

I'll never forget what one kid said, "This is why I don't go to church."

It's a terrible thing to take an exciting message like the gospel and make it BORING!

Watch out for the guy who's a walking sleeping pill. He's not the guy you want speaking at your next outreach program.

You Mean…These Are NOT Christians?

I'll never forget the time I brought almost 50 students to an event I trusted, only to find out that the speaker didn't know who he was talking to.

The purpose of the event was outreach. I knew it, the programmers knew it, the participating churches knew it, even most of the teenagers knew it. Students had brought their friends to hear the gospel. But instead, they heard a challenge to Christian kids.

Allow me to clarify. There's a definite need for good teaching that challenges Christian kids and motivates them to live for Christ. But there's also a definite *time* for this kind of talk, and that time is *not* during an outreach event.

Hundreds of outreach kids were packed into the chairs. The speaker was funny at first, and the students actually seemed to enjoy themselves. But then he started speaking a different language: "Some of us need to think about our walk with our savior."

At first the phrase flew right over my students' heads. They were used to teachers saying things they didn't understand. It flew by me the first time, too, probably because I'm used to church language. I didn't even catch it.

But then he kept saying it: "Our walk with our savior."

My students looked at each other and said, "Think about my 'walk'? What the he--?"

It got worse.

I don't remember much of his talk, but I'll always remember point number three: "Ask yourself, *What would Jesus do?*"

At this point I wanted to stand up and yell to this guy, "Hey, my kids don't even know Jesus! How are they gonna ask what he would do?"

I've seen it happen probably a hundred times. The speaker doesn't know how to talk to outreach kids. Or even worse, the speaker was never even told it was an outreach event.

In chapter 2 we defined an outreach event, so we need to make sure our speakers understand both our purpose and our audience. *They don't know Jesus, so don't treat them like they do!*

Often the problem lies with whoever booked the speaker. A few months ago a local youth guy was asked to speak at a campus outreach club near my house. The person who asked this guy to talk just said, "Can you come and speak at our campus outreach club?"

The speaker probably made some assumptions. He heard the words *campus* and *club* and assumed he'd be speaking at a Bible club. So he prepared a talk geared toward a handful of Christian kids.

When he got there, he was surprised to see so many "Christian kids." (Little did he know...) He gave a 20-minute talk on "How to reach out to the lost." The guy who was in charge of the outreach club was dying the whole time.

"Pssssst. Stop talking about the lost. They're right here!"

We need to book speakers who understand our audience, and we need to make sure we communicate with them clearly.

The "Christian" Palm Reader

I thought it was only on television. You know the guy. He stands in front of his television studio audience, closes his eyes, and starts twitching like he's having small convulsions. "I feel… I feel someone in the audience who is going through some intense sorrow right now."

Wow, that really narrows it down.

"The sorrow has to do with your…your father. Yes, your father!"

Think about it. How many people in this world are going through some emotional pain because of their dad? A ton! This isn't a mind reader—this is just a guy who reads *Newsweek.*

I didn't think I'd ever see it live, but I've seen it numerous times. It always happens during the invitation. The speaker tries to get people to come forward, and all of a sudden he turns into a mind reader.

Of course this person will usually spiritualize it by saying something like, "The Spirit is telling me…"

(Let me be clear. I'm not knocking people who are charismatic or believe in "the gifts." A good friend who writes for our ministry believes the gifts are for today, but she wouldn't be caught playing this palm reader game. And regardless of what any of us believe about the gifts, this fact remains: The use of any spiritual gift should point to God, not to ourselves. I believe the Spirit can reveal things to us, but let's be honest—the world doesn't need our tricks. The world needs the truth of the gospel. The world needs Jesus. So let's give Jesus to them.)

SCREENING YOUR SPEAKERS

Let me save you a lot of pain. If there's one truth I want you to get out of this chapter, just read these three words: **Screen your speakers!**

That's right. Don't use a speaker you don't know about firsthand. Don't use a speaker if you haven't heard him speak or if he hasn't been recommended by people you trust. Take the time and make the effort to choose a good speaker who'll help you accomplish what God's leading you to do through your event.

Here are a few steps I take whenever I book a speaker. And when I do, I rarely get burned:

1. Listen to the speaker yourself. I like booking speakers I've heard before, especially if they're "unknown." I want to hear if a person is gifted at speaking and scripturally solid. I want to hear how he handles a crowd. I want to know if he's funny, powerful, or relevant. I must admit, I haven't always listened to a speaker first. If the speaker is known in the youth ministry world, one time in 10 I'd just listen to word-of-mouth referrals. And I don't mean a vague, "People say he's pretty good..." I want to hear recommendations from people I know and trust who say this speaker really came through for their event. This leads me to the second step.

2. Check the speaker's references. Even if you've heard the speaker before, it's still a good idea to check some of her references. I like to talk to a few people who've booked her for other events so I can find out if she was easy to work with and if she did what she was asked to do. If I haven't heard the speaker before, then I'm going to check her references for sure. I'll sometimes ask a speaker for the names of contact people from her last three speaking engagements. That way I'm getting recent references from people who've used this person before.

3. Communicate with the speaker in person.
I always want to talk to the speaker personally. However, many speakers use booking agents. That's fine for negotiating dates and prices, but I still want to talk with a speaker before I hire him. If I can't talk with the speaker I'm booking, then I won't book him.

When I do talk with a potential speaker, I clearly communicate what I'm looking for in a speaker. I tell him about my event and the expected audience. I also give him a rough idea of the program and ask him if he thinks he's a good fit.

If at the end of the conversation, the speaker agrees and you book him, then make sure you clearly communicate your event's purpose and any important logistical details both orally and in writing. Make sure the speaker understands how long he's supposed to speak and what he should do when he's finished speaking.

I don't micro-manage my speakers. Once I've gone through the initial steps to book them, I let them use their gifts as God leads. I've already shared the parameters they need to know. They understand the purpose; and they understand their allotted time and other logistics. I never ask to look at their talks beforehand or offer criticisms of their outlines. If I need to do that with a speaker, then I've booked the wrong one.

The only thing I do that might be received as "overly thorough" is clarifying the important details as the event gets closer. I understand the importance of doing this from my own speaking engagements. Sometimes I'm booked as far ahead as a year in advance for some programs, camps, or events. That means I'll have spoken to 40 other crowds between the time I was booked and the time I actually speak.

So I review the details of a specific event with my speaker one week prior and again on the day of the actual program or event, just to remind her of the important details: The audience, the purpose, the theme, and the exact time she's been allotted to speak.

It's Not Easy

It's not easy speaking to an outreach crowd. I remember when I started a campus ministry and began speaking to 150 to 200 students in the bleachers of a junior high school on Wednesday nights. It was one of the most difficult things I've ever experienced. 90 percent of them didn't go to church; they just showed up to our campus event because it was fun. The last thing they wanted to do was hear someone preach. So I typically had about 20 seconds to catch these teenagers' attention. If I didn't have them by then, I was dead in the water.

Once I had their attention, I had to keep it. I had to be relevant, speaking to the struggles, questions, and feelings of emptiness in their lives. I learned how to use lots of stories and examples. I learned how to use humor—usually at my own expense.

If I'm looking for a speaker for my outreach event, I don't want to bring in someone who's inexperienced or just learning how to speak. Large outreach events are not a training ground for new speakers. Outreach speakers need to be relevant, they need to grab the students' attention, and they need to keep it for the length of the talk. (There are some great books and training materials available for people who want to better their speaking skills. I highly recommend the *Dynamic Communicator Workshop* put on by either Ken Davis or Jay Laffoon. Jump on my Web site, www.TheSourceForYouthMinistry.com, for more of these recommended resources, as well as some speaker references.)

Speakers can have a huge impact on our events, so we need to be very careful when selecting them. The speaker often carries the burden of the entire purpose of the event: Sharing the gospel. Thus, it would be foolish for us to spend hours preparing funny videos, wild games, and extravagant sets, but only dedicate a few minutes to booking a speaker.

bypassing bands that just don't "get it"...

...and booking bands that do

About 4,000 students gathered in the outdoor arena. Some had driven for nearly three hours and then stood in line for an additional two. Three big-name Christian bands were booked, and church youth groups had been encouraged to bring their friends to listen to some music and hear the gospel. The event's focus was outreach.

The organization that planned the event told the bands about its purpose: "We want to show students that music can be clean and fun. But most of all, we want to share the gospel and give kids an opportunity to respond."

A speaker had been flown in and was now waiting for the third band to finish their set. Over 100 trained counselors with bright yellow counselor badges were ready and waiting with Bibles in hand.

So far the event was an incredible success. The crowd loved the bands, and even after hours of standing, jumping, moshing, and screaming, they seemed to want more.

The last band did their final number, and we waited in anticipation for the big introduction. The band was going to invite the speaker to come onstage, introduce him, and then sit in some chairs onstage right, just in view of the audience. Their very presence was going to speak volumes to the audience, as if they were saying, *We think this is important enough for us to sit here and listen, too.*

This was the plan. And it was a pretty good one at that.

But it didn't happen.

The band finished their final song and said, "Thank you very much! Come see us again!" Exit stage left.

Silence. Then the crowd started to exit as well. The counselors looked at each other in confusion.

That's when I saw the guy in charge of the event running down one of the side aisles toward the stage. He leaped onstage and ran to the center microphone. He tried to talk—but the sound was turned off. The speaker now wandered onto the stage as well.

Not many noticed—they were all headed toward the exits. After all, it had been a three-hour event so far. By the time the microphone was turned back on, about 300 people had exited.

"Wait!"

Everyone stopped and looked toward the stage. (Well, 3,700 people stopped anyway.)

"It's not over!" The man onstage pleaded. "We've still got a speaker that you're going to want to hear." Then he stumbled over his words, unprepared for the dropped baton and still catching his breath from the leap onto the stage. Yet he somehow managed to introduce the speaker.

You could see it on their faces. Those who were halfway to the exits were looking at each other, debating, *Do we stay or do we go?* It was a debate that wouldn't have been an issue if the band had done what they were supposed to do. But it was too late now—hundreds more exited.

One small but crucial blunder, and they lost more than 1,000 people.

BLAME IT ON COMMUNICATION

I was standing there with my bright yellow counselor's badge, and my jaw dropped to the ground. I saw the whole thing fall apart right before my eyes.

The next day I saw my buddy who was in charge of the event. "How did it happen?" I asked him curiously.

"I don't know. We talked to them about it 100 times."

"You talked to the band?" I prodded.

"Well, their manager," my buddy said sheepishly. "We never really talked to the band. The manager handles all the communication."

Or does he?

I can't emphasize this point enough: Communicate with the *band*. Don't assume they know what you're doing. Don't assume they remember the conversation you had with them on the phone six months ago. They've done more than 20 gigs since then.

THE THREE BAND "BOO BOOS"

There are three major areas of misunderstanding when it comes to working with bands on an event.

They Don't See the Big Picture

"Come back! There's gonna be some skits and stuff."

That's what the lead singer actually said. It's burned in my brain forever.

We'd booked the local sports arena, and more than 5,000 students showed up. We brought a speaker who'd spoken in school assemblies all week. At each and every assembly, he invited the students to attend our arena event at the end of the week.

Churches drove from around the state to come to the event. The publicity said, "Bring unchurched kids!" Teenagers of all colors, shapes, and sizes had filled the arena.

The speaker had been in a gang, served time in jail, and had been shot several times before he found Christ. His testimony was very powerful.

The band was a huge Christian band. You probably have one of their CDs in your collection. Many churches came just to hear the band.

The draw had worked.

The program was all planned out: The band would start off the event. Then a short drama would be followed by a dance routine by an inner-city youth group. Finally, our speaker would present the gospel—the very reason we put on the event.

Supposedly the band had been prepped. "The purpose of this event is outreach. Our speaker is going to present the gospel and give an invitation."

"Great!" they replied sincerely while tuning their guitars. "What time are we on again?"

We showed them the schedule one more time.

The event started with a roar, and students blissfully bounced around the arena to the deafening wail of the guitar. Everything was going as planned.

The band finished their set, and all they had to do was walk off stage so the drama could start on the opposite side. The band didn't even have to introduce the drama—just finish playing their final song and exit. Simple, right? Finish and exit.

Not even close.

"That's all we have for you today," the lead singer said, while breathing heavily into the microphone and wiping the sweat from his forehead. "Thanks for coming out!" he continued, "We'll be standing in the back by our table full of CDs and T-shirts—signing autographs!"

And then 10 seconds too late, the band exited stage left.

Everyone in the arena started to exit as well. After all, "That's all they have for us today."

That's when I saw my boss escorting the lead singer back onstage, like a second grader who'd been caught putting a frog in a girl's desk. The flustered band member quickly grabbed the microphone and yelled to the crowd, "Wait!"

Those who hadn't already exited the arena stopped in the aisles and turned to listen.

And that's when he said it: "Come back! There's gonna be some skits and stuff."

To this day I still tease my former boss about that comment. Whenever we're talking about a gospel presentation at an event—the entire purpose of the evening—we call it "skits and stuff."

If the band doesn't understand the big picture, it won't matter how many times you tell them what to do and when to do it. They'll miss the target as loose cannons often do.

Remember this when booking a band. Talk with them and see if they understand the big idea. If they don't understand, then don't book 'em. No band is worth missing the entire purpose of your event.

But there are other areas of misunderstanding when it comes to working with bands for an event.

They Don't See the Importance of Time

The gymnasium was filled with a little more than 1,000 teenagers. The event was held at the local high school three evenings in a row. Publicity was phenomenal. The school had several on-campus Christian organizations involved, and they'd invited every type of kid imaginable: Every jock, every druggie, every math whiz—you name it, they were there.

The program seemed to be well planned. Two hilarious high school students performed a funny skit, a few prizes were given away, the band performed, and then it was my turn.

The purpose of the event was to share the gospel. I was allotted 25 minutes to speak, five minutes for an altar call, and 15 minutes for counseling. Counselors were ready and all the ducks seemed to be sitting neatly in a row.

Then the band played…

and played…

and played…

and played…

does this feel like a Dr. Seuss book yet?

Well then, let me tell you how I felt:

My name is Jon.

I'm supposed to be on.

Jon isn't on because the time is now gone.

To help you understand the situation, let's use some of the skills we learned earlier in this book. Let's plan from the end of the event backward.

The event was scheduled to end at 8:30 PM, so we needed to be prepared for the exit of 1,000 students at that time. A good programmer would stop and think about how that exit would take place. This event was geared for seventh through twelfth graders, many of whom can't drive. So, four out of the six grade levels in attendance (about 650 students) will *need rides home*. The majority of these students will get rides from parents.

Follow my logic for a moment: The speaker and the altar call were the last items on the agenda. If the parents of more than 600 students show up around 8:30 PM to pick up their kids, then we don't want to keep them waiting.

Now think about the kinds of students this type of event is supposed to draw. This group did such a fantastic job with marketing that they drew a ton of unchurched kids from the campus. Therefore, the unchurched parents of 600 students will be arriving to pick up their children at 8:30. Do you want to keep them waiting? Do you want to run so late that these parents angrily show up at the door to look for their kids, only to see adults praying with their children in a corner?

As you can see, we don't want to run late with our counseling time. It might even be a good idea to shoot to finish the counseling time at 8:25, just to be safe. And since we want our counselors to have at least 15 minutes with the students, it would probably be good to make sure that the five-minute altar call happens at 8:05 so the counselors can start meeting with the students at 8:10, which means they should be done well before 8:30.

Now, let's continue to work backward.

If we need to begin our altar call at 8:05, and our speaker needs 25 minutes to speak, then he should start speaking at 7:40—correct?

That was the plan.

But as the band played on, the clock rolled forward. 7:40 passed. 7:50 passed. I watched the clock turn to eight o'clock. The event coordinators started giving the "cut it" sign to the band from the front row. But the band was a little too caught up in their music to notice. At 8:08, I was finally introduced. According to the schedule, I was supposed to have started my altar call three minutes ago. I now had two minutes to tell kids about Jesus and get them out the door.

Highly improbable.

Needless to say, there wasn't any counseling that night. I spoke for 12 minutes and gave an invitation for them to raise their hands. Then I implored them to come back the next evening. By God's grace, we had a fabulous response of raised hands. But it disappointed us that they didn't have the opportunity to meet with counselors one-on-one as planned.

The event coordinators were livid. I was too. We talked to the band, and they apologized enthusiastically. We all went home exhausted; we had two more nights of this.

Now it's night number two. And 7:40 passed by again. Then 7:50.

Not again.

I was introduced at 7:58. Yes, I had seven minutes to present the gospel and start my altar call. Then during the counseling, I was going to go commit murder backstage!

Despite the band and in spite of my bitterness, God worked. I spoke for about 11 minutes and gave the quickest altar call in history. We got students out the door with counselors, and we prayed they'd be quick.

That night the leader of the event had a little talk with the band. It wasn't pretty. But what amazed me was the band's absolute lack of respect for the schedule. *What's the big deal?* They didn't care about being late, so they assumed everyone else felt the same way. *You should have just run late!* To this day, they're probably still wondering why "those people" (we) were so uptight about time.

Don't book a band that isn't conscious of their time limits. If your team has carefully planned out everything down to the last minute, then a band who oversteps the time boundaries could endanger the whole purpose of the event. Don't let a band sacrifice your purpose.

They Don't See the Audience

The purpose of the event was outreach, but the band decided to lead worship instead. This wouldn't have been so bad if the guy who was leading it didn't put everyone to sleep after 30 minutes.

After 25 minutes he put down his guitar, and we all thought, "Good, he's done." But he just picked up another guitar and said, "Can you feel this? I really feel something happening here. Isn't it awesome to just worship God?"

I still don't know what he felt up there onstage. Maybe it was indigestion. Everyone in the room was sure bored out of their skulls. I wish I'd had a video camera on me. The nonverbal cues of the audience members were screaming, *"Please shut up!"*

And guess who was next? Yep. About 30 more minutes into the coma, it was my turn to speak. It took me seven minutes just to wake up the audience.

As a speaker, one of the first things I learned was to notice the nonverbal cues of the audience. Every time I speak at a school assembly, during the first two minutes I see the nonverbal cues of hundreds of teenagers asking me, *"Why should I listen to you?"* I then have about 20 seconds to address that question, or I'll lose them. And if I see them drifting, I have to bring them back again.

Sometimes people will ask me to speak very late at night at camps. During those times I absolutely must consider the audience and the late hour, and then use their nonverbal cues as a guide to whether or not I'm getting through.

And musicians—even if they're leading worship—need to do the same.

One of the biggest ways we alienate people during outreach programs is through worship. It sounds odd—maybe even a bit harsh—but think about it: If we're trying to draw a huge crowd of students who don't believe in Jesus, why would we book a band that's trying to get teenagers to sing praises to God?

If a worship band got booked to sing in a bar, do you think they should start by saying, "Come on now, everybody sing along with this one! Here I am to worship. Here I am to bow down..."

Good luck.

I'm not saying you can't do worship at outreach events. Willow Creek and Young Life have been pulling it off for years. As a matter of fact, they do a fantastic job at it. But if you do decide to use worship for your outreach event, *don't* let the worship leader start off by saying, "Are you guys ready to praise Jesus?" Some members of the crowd might simply be there because of the free pizza. After all, that's what the flyer said.

If you decide to do some worship, then try saying something like this: "Praising God with music is something we like to do around here. Feel free to join us or listen in—we're just glad you're here with us today."

And be careful with the time. The worship I've seen work at outreach events has always been short. Unfortunately, the majority of it isn't.

Once I spoke at a youth rally where they'd invited the whole town to the local community center. The purpose was outreach, and they expected a ton of unchurched people to attend.

The guy in charge of the event really had some good ideas—I was excited about the event. But then I found out he was also the worship leader. I didn't want to make any rash judgments, but it was difficult. Rule of thumb: If the worship leader is in charge of the event, then that means you can expect a *long* worship time.

He showed me the program agenda and reminded me that I was speaking right after the worship band.

"Great," I said, putting a piece of gum in my mouth and trying not to be skeptical. "How many songs are you guys singing?"

"Thirteen," he said.

I almost swallowed my gum.

I'll say it again: *Remember your audience. They don't know Jesus, so don't treat them like they do!*

And if a band can't seem to do that, then don't book them to begin with.

WHEN BOOKING A BAND

Here are four steps to follow when you want to book a band without getting burned.

Listen to the Band *in Concert*

Almost every place I speak has booked a band as well. I always ask the event planners, "Have you used this band before?"

Ninety percent say, "No, this is the first time I've heard them."

Very often a band will do something or say something that makes the event coordinators squirm. I'm usually standing with these people when it happens. Sometimes I ask, "Did you know they were going to do this?"

"No!" they quickly respond. "We had no idea!"

Of course they had no idea. They'd never heard the band perform before.

I remember hearing a band where the lead singer talked for five to 10 minutes before every song. The band's music was great—if only the lead singer would shut up and play the next song already. As it was, they played way longer than the time allotted.

Of course the people who booked his band said, "I had no idea he was going to do this!"

I nonchalantly asked the band's sound guy, "Does he always talk like this between songs?" The sound guy said, "Oh yeah. He loves to speak to the kids. He does it all the time!"

Of course, the group who booked the band didn't know this, but anyone who'd ever heard that band perform live sure did.

Go listen to the band in concert. Their CD doesn't tell you how they perform live, even if it's a live CD (it's always edited in some way). Find out if they keep to their allotted time, and if they do what's requested of them.

Check References

Talk to people who've recently booked the band. Don't just talk to three of the lead singer's best friends. Ask for a list of the last five people who booked them. Make sure you talk to at least one person who booked them for an event that's similar to what you're planning to do. Ask the person if the band kept to the time schedule. Ask if the band did what they were asked to do. References can tell you a lot about a band. Don't check just one. Check several. There are two sides to every story, but if you call three to five references, you'll soon find the common denominator.

Communicate with the Actual Band Members

Clear communication of your goal begins when you first book a band.

Reality: Most Christian bands are used to playing to Christian crowds. They're used to beginning their sets by yelling, "Is everyone ready to praise Jesus?"

Ask the band if they've played for many outreach events. Ask them what kind of performance they'd do if they invited their unchurched friends to their concert. Would they talk differently? Would they ask their unbelieving friends, "Are you ready to praise Jesus?"

Clearly communicate the purpose of your event to them. Let them know that you want to point students to Jesus and explain how you're going to do it. Let them know your method. Explain to them "if and when" the gospel is going to be shared. And if someone is going to share the gospel, then tell the band how much time the speaker needs to do so.

Regardless of how many times you've talked with the band, always talk to them again "one week out" and "the day of." "One week out" because that way they can plan their set appropriately for the purpose of your event. And on "the day of," just to make sure they remember. Almost every time a band blows it at an outreach event, it's because of miscommunication. Somehow, the band didn't understand.

Use a Contract

Contracts are a good idea. They allow you to put into writing all the important elements you want to communicate with the band.

If the most important element of your event is the transition between the band and the speaker, put that in the contract. Clearly outline that the band will not plug their CD table, nor preach a sermon, but they're to finish their set, introduce the speaker, and sit on the side of the stage while the speaker talks.

I knew a guy who was so fed up with bands that he put all of these elements into the contract. If the band didn't do these things, then they didn't get paid. Contracts keep the bands accountable to what you've discussed.

THERE ARE BANDS YOU CAN COUNT ON

In general, though, bands are not the enemy. I've worked with many, many bands full of humble servants who are reliable, flexible, and gracious! These bands are a joy to work with. They see the big picture of the event, they want to be a part of the team, and they're fantastic to minister with. They lead worship with songs that kids know and a few that they quickly grow to love. They have incredible character and truly point to God, not themselves. They are 2 Corinthians 4:5 in action. That's why I recommend them on our Web page.

So don't book just any band. Find a band you can count on. Book a band that will help you achieve the purpose of your event.

They're out there, and they want to help you reach teenagers with the life-changing message of Jesus Christ.

bypassing bands that just don't "get it" ...

slam dunks
10 outreach programs and events that work

So you've read the "how tos," but now some of you are asking, "What really works?"

Good question. What are some events that actually apply these theories we've been talking about?

Here are the top 10 "slam dunks" I've observed—outreach ideas I've seen work over and over again when people put time and planning into them. These are NOT the only events that work, but hopefully these ideas will get your mental gears turning a little bit.

Please understand—your event might flop big time if you try to simply duplicate one of these events and forget the event-planning process I've outlined in this book. The ideas I share below only worked because someone noticed a need in their area and took the time and did the necessary planning to meet that need with these programs or events.

Remember, no one knows the teenagers in your area better than you do. The best thing you can do is continue to get to know your area, learn what students like to do, align your draw with their interests—and watch God work.

With that in mind, here are 10 "slam dunks" that give you an idea about the kinds of events that work.

1. WAREHOUSE EXTREME

Youth for Christ hosts an annual junior high event in the Sacramento, California area. They rent a huge warehouse and fill it with every inflatable activity imaginable: Sumo suits, jousting pits, boxing rings, climbing walls, bungee runs, giant slides, obstacle courses, and any new items that came out that year. Junior high kids love this stuff. Some of us who've been in youth ministry for years might tire of it, but seventh and eighth graders don't.

This event also features areas with basketball competitions, hockey, skateboarding, and carnival events. The warehouse is filled with more activities than you can imagine. All this and a giant liability policy!

The event started years ago with only a handful of churches in attendance and only a few inflatables. But as the word got out, the event grew. Within five years the event was drawing 800 students, each paying $10. This gave Youth for Christ the budget to bring out plenty of attractions and quality speakers.

The agenda is this: Students enjoy all the activities from 7 to 10 PM. At 10 PM the YFC staffers shut down the events and herd everyone over to a stage area (with more than 1,000 chairs set up) for a quick program.

This is always a tricky situation. They tell 1,000 junior highers to stop playing on the fun stuff and sit in a chair. As you may have predicted, this can be difficult. But it's necessary because the quick program features the purpose of the event: A speaker who presents the gospel. They know it takes about 15 minutes to get everyone moved over. And to the person running the event, it always feels like the longest 15 minutes of his life. It's what I call the "vital 15." Those 15 minutes are the most important 15 minutes of the entire evening.

Youth for Christ quickly learned they had to have an exciting "attraction" happening up on the stage during those 15 minutes before the program begins. This attraction during the "vital 15" had to accomplish two things: 1) It had to attract students (making it easier for all the event staff who were herding 1,000 teenagers), and 2) It had to keep the students' interest while everyone gathered.

When I used to run this event, one of the most successful elements I used for the "vital 15" was a rapper/beat-boxer friend of mine named Maximillian (that's why I still recommend him on my Web site). Max can make any sound with his mouth, and when he gets going, he sounds like a drum machine. Regardless of what kind of music students liked, they always found Max fascinating. For years I used Max to work the microphone for the "vital 15." Everyone seemed eager to get over to the stage area to see him; and by the start of our program, everyone's eyes were glued to the stage.

Then at 10:15 we began our quick program. The speaker got up onstage immediately and gave an invitation by 10:45 (so the counselors would have 15 minutes with the students). The event was over at 11 PM.

In recent years they've made a programming switch where they do the program first and then the activities. This has helped eliminate the intense pressure of the "vital 15." Good programs will always make adjustments like this to try to improve.

This event has been bringing out about 1,000 kids and staff for years, and it often yields hundreds of teenagers who make decisions for Christ.

2. SLAM-DUNK SHOWDOWN

Basketball is a huge draw. And everyone who loves basketball loves to watch a good slam dunk.

Slam-dunk contests are a great way to attract the whole community. You not only attract the competitors, but you also attract the people who want to watch.

To run the event, you need a location with good seating— a gymnasium is perfect. You'll also need several adjustable basketball hoops. Most portable basketball hoops are adjustable these days.

Some people like to run the competition with several categories: The seven-foot division, the eight-foot division, and a nine-foot division. It's also good to have clear guidelines for who can enter which division. Most people who run an event like this will allow any teenager to enter, but with a high school and junior high division.

Most people have watched the NBA Dunk Contest, where all the contestants perform three dunks, judges give each contestant a score, and then the "top dunkers" go on to a final championship round. It's good to model the NBA contest since many students are familiar with it.

This is a great opportunity to invite the entire community to your event. The more you market it, the more people you'll attract. If you have contacts with schools or coaches, they can also serve as great publicity for this type of event.

It works best when you charge little or no admission price for the audience, but just charge a small entry fee for the dunkers. The dunkers will invite their families and friends to watch, and the word spreads rapidly.

Program length will vary with the number of dunkers who compete, but usually the time slot just before the championship round is a good time to introduce a speaker.

Celebrity speakers will increase the draw of the event. Numerous cities have Christian NBA players who are open to speaking at this kind of event. Don't say *no* for someone. He can't say *yes* if you don't ask him.

3. SKATENIGHT

Skateboarding events bring out a totally different group of teenagers than basketball events. But that's good. As I said before, diverse methods reach a diverse group of students.

A buddy of mine named Andy started a skateboard outreach at a local church. Andy said he was tired of hearing about how people in churches would chase away skateboarders.

I knew what he was talking about. Our church janitor hung up No Skateboarding signs, and he'd get irate—literally red in the face—every time he saw a skateboarder on church property. "These kids have NO respect for our church property. They grind their boards on our bricks. I had to replace three bricks last month!"

I understand his frustration, but I'm not sure I agree with his response. Neither did my friend Andy.

Andy put a huge sign on the street corner in front of the church: Skaters Welcome Tuesday Nights. Then on Tuesday night he rolled a couple of skateboard ramps into the church parking lot.

A handful of skateboarders came out the first time. They couldn't believe a church was allowing them to skate on the property.

Andy raised some funds and built some more ramps and grinding bars. He even invested in a bunch of skateboard helmets. He developed a system where students could come and skate, but they had to wear a helmet. If they didn't have one, Andy would provide one.

Within two months Andy had a problem. About 200 students were showing up in the parking lot on Tuesdays—a good problem to have. He had to quickly recruit more staff and raise funds for more ramps and helmets.

Andy ran his Skatenight from 7 to 9 PM on Tuesday nights. At 8 PM he'd always stop everything and make people take a seat on their helmets. He'd talk for 10 minutes and just share what Christ was doing in his life. Then at 8:10, everyone could skate again.

It was that simple. And some of those skaters started showing up at church on Sunday mornings.

4. AFTER-PROM PARTY

Let's face it. Numerous things happen on prom night that students live to regret later in life. Maybe some of the pressure to do these things is because of a lack of positive options after the prom.

Years ago a youth pastor in Colorado submitted an idea to our ministry's Web site about an after-prom party. I thought the idea was great, and since that time I've seen several youth ministries do this kind of event.

Publicize it like any other event. Think of some unique items that will draw your students to the event: Food, live music, and plenty of places to hang out. Some groups have done midnight barbeques or pizza. Others have set up a movie area with a ton of couches for students to sit and watch. A few inflatable activities—like the big-time boxing rings or sumo suits—might add some fun. Two girls boxing in their prom dresses would make a great promo picture for a future flyer and the youth room wall.

You could also run this event like the all-night event (#10 below) with various activities or locations. You wouldn't need to share the gospel or have a speaker. This is just a great event to bring out new students and invite them back to church. Regardless, this event provides a fun, clean, drug- and alcohol-free environment for teenagers to hang out.

The pastor in Colorado who originally suggested the idea to our Web site ran the event from midnight until six in the morning. They had a few hundred students show up.

5. HOOP'N THREE-ON-THREE

Hoop'n Three-on-Three is a great way to draw out basketball players, as well as anyone else who wants to watch. Find a facility where you can set up several basketball courts. A large gym with multiple courts is best. You can even run half-court for these three-on-three tournaments.

Publicize the event much like you would the slam-dunk event. Drop off flyers at various basketball practices around the community. Contact every basketball coach you know, and see if they'll publicize it for you.

Charge an entry fee for each team and have a minimal cover charge for people in the audience. Provide a snack bar—a must at any event that lasts this long. It's also another way to pay for some of the costs of the event.

Start the tournament in the afternoon and play "sudden death." If a team loses, they're out. Depending on the number of teams, the event will probably last for hours.

Run the final championship game full-court. Use the time just before the final game to have a speaker give a brief talk. Or use the time just before the trophy ceremony. Just consider this: The more teams you include in the ceremony, the bigger the audience you'll have when the speaker shares.

6. FIFTH QUARTER PARTY

It's Friday night and the fourth quarter of the football game comes to a close. Every teenager in this small town looks at each other and says, "What're we gonna do after?"

Make the Fifth Quarter Party the place to be.

I recently spoke in a small town in Tennessee where the high school sits right across the street from a small church. The youth meet in a barn behind the church midweek, and on Friday nights, music is pumped out of that barn for a Fifth Quarter Party.

Students walk in the room to find several kegs full of— root beer. Yes, root beer. All–you-can-drink root beer for $1, and all-you-can-eat pizza for $2. There are two pool tables, a ping-pong table, foosball, and an Xbox on two different giant screen TVs.

A local teen center near my hometown runs Fifth Quarter Parties after every football and basketball game at the school down the street, attracting up to 1,000 kids on a Friday night. Youth pastors from five different area churches use this event as an opportunity to hang out with kids and meet new students. Local law enforcement hangs out at the center as well. (They get free food and soft drinks.)

A group from a small church in Iowa sent in a similar idea to our Web site, and they now draw up to 300 seventh through twelfth graders every Friday night.

slam dunks

7. CONCERT FESTIVAL

Battle of the Bands, Concert Fest, Youth Awakening—I've heard it called many things. The basic elements of this event are multiple bands and a speaker.

One thing to consider when doing this type of event is "transitions." Multiple bands usually mean a lot of dead time when you're changing from one band to the next. Always ask yourself, "What will keep the kids there?"

I've been to all-day events or even weekend events where this was not a problem. As long as more bands are coming, that fact seems to keep students in attendance. Just be careful when the last band is playing. Some people will take this opportunity to duck out early. If you plan to use a speaker, take this into consideration. You might want to schedule the speaker somewhere in the middle of the agenda, rather than at the end.

Sometimes you can find a band where one of the members is a good speaker. This is a great situation. Usually this guy will have already earned the students' respect. The students are already tuned in—he just needs to *not* lose their attention. Don't just ask the band if any of them also speak. Almost every band has someone who *thinks* he's a speaker. I'd only use someone I've heard before and trust.

But I'll be honest: When the speaker *is* a person from the band, that means one less transition. And the fewer transitions there are the better. Transitions are where you lose people.

And make sure you don't book just any band. Really observe what music styles teenagers in your community listen to. Ask around and find out what bands that play that genre of music can deliver.

Music is a huge draw for teenagers today. If you can provide an event with bands students want to hear, you'll be amazed by the results.

8. JELL-O WRESTLING

That's right. Jell-O wrestling.

Here's how you do it: Find a store that sells bulk foods and purchase large quantities of instant Jell-O—enough to make 80 gallons. You can make it in a bunch of large (*new*) rubber or plastic garbage cans and then let the Jell-O set up in a big walk-in refrigerator.

Some of us may not have access to a walk-in fridge, or we don't have a connection with a local grocery store that will let us use their milk fridge. But our options aren't all dried up. There are some places on the Internet that sell an instant "no chill" Jell-O. It's a lot more expensive, but it's another option.

Once you make (or buy) the Jell-O, scoop it into baby pools and you're ready to go. It's just like normal wrestling, but in Jell-O and within the confines of a baby pool. It's slick, and it's wrestling, so use caution and discernment.

My buddy did this several times with his small ministry. His normal attendance was about 12 to 15 students a week, but he'd have 40 to 50 students show up on Jell-O Wrestling night. He told the students to wear clothes that could get messy, and he also did the event outside for easier clean up. (Note: I said "easier," not "easy.")

I prefer guys versus guys and girls versus girls. This lessens the chance of injury and inappropriate physical contact.

Sometimes modesty can also be an issue. One way to solve that problem is to buy a large number of XXL T-shirts in two different colors. Make every wrestler put on a T-shirt over their clothes—each one wearing a different color.

Events like this could bring out a ton of new students. I use them to show kids that our church group is fun and then invite them back. If you videotape the event, even more students will return the next week to watch the highlights.

slam dunks

9. MUD BOWL

During every one of my high school years, my church hosted a huge Mud Bowl—a giant, co-ed touch football game in a muddy field.

I've seen a ton of youth groups do this type of event. One group would actually plow a field with soft dirt and then water it down for a week before the game.

The sky's the limit with this idea. You can play football, rugby—even freeze tag, where fellow players have to dive between their teammate's legs to unfreeze them.

This is a great event for your students to invite their friends to come along. Make sure you take some video footage during the game because you'll have a perfect "greatest hits" video that you can use to draw people back the next week.

A group in New Jersey sent in a similar idea to our Web site. They play it every year and provide Mud Bowl T-shirts to each attendee with a youth group motto on it.

10. KICKIN' IT ALL NIGHT

It's an all-night party with plenty of activities and plenty of time to hang out or just "kick it." After all, one of a teenager's favorite things to do is just "kick it."

You could almost market it as just that. Picture it:

KICKIN' IT
CALVARY YOUTH'S ALL-NIGHT PARTY

Plenty of Stuff to Do—and Plenty of Time to Just Kick It!

Just plan activities for the entire night, starting at your normal meeting place. Then go to different fun places where teenagers can participate or simply hang out. I've done a lot of these all-nighters, and they're always a hit.

This event requires enough vehicles to haul your entire group around, enough drivers who can handle driving all night, and enough coffee to help keep the drivers awake! Start at your normal facility with either an open gym or some fun organized games. After a couple of hours, switch to the next location.

I've done this with 30 to 40 students. Believe it or not, I've also done it as a citywide event with 1,200 to 1,400 students.

For just 30 or 40 students, I'd often start at a church gym with a bunch of games and good food with lots of sugar and caffeine. Then we'd pile into vehicles and head off to our next location.

Possible Locations/Activities

• Laser Tag

• Bowling (especially at a place that does "black light" bowling)

• Swimming (at a person's house, a neighborhood pool, or even a local hotel, if prearranged)

• Movie (I have a friend who has a fancy home theatre in his house)

• Roller Skating

• Ice Skating/Broom Hockey

• Teen Centers (Youth for Christ has a teen center in our city with pool tables, ping pong, air hockey, etc.)

slam dunks

Usually, I'd close the event by ending somewhere for breakfast.

This event always attracted a large number of students; but because of transportation needs, we had to limit our numbers. I offered door prizes and prizes for students who brought a friend. I often used this event to attract new students to our group and invite them back to future events. I rarely included a program.

However, at the huge citywide event with 1,200 to 1,400 teenagers, we always used this opportunity to run a program and present the gospel. We'd start off with a huge program at a church followed by pizza. Then individual churches (they provided their own transportation) would go to one of three main locations: Roller skating, laser tag, or a mini-golf place. Sound logistically difficult? Not really. We just did the math of how many people could fit at each location. Some years we rented out three laser-tag locations, two skating rinks, and two mini-golf locations. When people registered at the beginning of the evening, we gave them a schedule of what locations they would attend at what time. We also gave them a map to each location.

Basically, we started at 10 PM, ran a program and ate pizza until about 11:30, and then people left for their different locations. We divided the midnight-to-6 AM time frame into three equal time slots: 12 to 2 AM, 2 to 4 AM, and 4 to 6 AM. Groups stayed at their first locations for about an hour and a half and then loaded up to arrive at their second locations at 2 AM. They arrived at their third and final locations at 4 AM, and then at 6 AM they all went straight home.

Logistically speaking, the most difficult part was check-in. We always needed a bright, organized individual in charge of placing the groups in certain slots. As groups checked in, some would be assigned "Skating, Laser Tag, and Mini Golf." Others would be "Laser Tag, Mini Golf, and Skating."

As the event got bigger and we added more locations, registration became even more confusing. Some teams would be "Skating Rink A, Laser-Tag Location C, and Mini Golf B." You can see why we needed a very organized person to handle this element.

The event was always a success, and we often had hundreds of students make decisions for Christ during the program at the beginning of the evening.

slam dunks

making it happen

where do we go from here?

Now it's your turn.

You've read the book, so now what? You have two choices:

1. Hope someone else will do it.

2. Make it happen.

THE LITTLE YOUTH LEADER WHO COULD

Once upon a time there was a little youth group. They lived in a tiny town with a small church and only one school, K-12. The youth group consisted of 12 students each week: The pastor's son, the head elder's daughter, eight other church kids, and two community kids who just showed up each week.

Sunday school was from 9:30 to 10:30 on Sunday mornings, followed by the church service. Wednesday nights were mandatory. It was said that if you missed Wednesday night, two of the head deacons made sure you lost your salvation.

This little youth group figured they could never do anything big. After all, they'd tried before and it didn't work. Years ago they planned an event and invited everyone they knew. The results weren't as positive as they'd expected, so the idea of future events was quickly stifled.

Sundays and Wednesdays continued unscathed, but the youth leaders secretly wished they could do something to reach out beyond the church walls. Unfortunately, the fear of failure lurked over their heads.

One day one of the youth leaders, a small quiet woman, saw a neighborhood boy riding his skateboard on church property. This was a common sight in their small town. Teenagers were always looking for places to skateboard. The leader felt something prompting her to act. She tried to ignore the feeling, but her stomach felt as though it were going to twist inside out. (Perhaps she shouldn't have stopped for fast food on the way to church that morning.) Pushing aside her anxiety, she walked over to the boy and began a conversation.

"You're pretty good on that skateboard."

The boy looked at her as if she were from another planet. "Huh?"

She swallowed and spoke a little louder, "I just said I thought you were pretty good on that skateboard there." She brushed her hair from her face, a little embarrassed.

The boy smirked a bit and pulled his pants up an inch or two so they rested uncomfortably halfway up his boxers (blue plaid—it was hard not to notice!). "Thanks," he said quickly, flipping the board with his feet and landing back on top, as surefooted as a cat.

"Is there anyplace to skate around here?" the youth leader asked, feeling a little braver than she'd felt a second ago.

This seemed to spark some interest in the boy. "No. The best place is the shopping center across the street, but they don't let us skate there." His forehead wrinkled. "And they've got a security guy who chases us off all the time."

The conversation continued, and the youth worker became a little more comfortable as each minute passed. The boy opened up even more as time went on. Then they finally said their goodbyes. Actually, she said, "Good-bye," and he said, "Later!"

The fire had been ignited.

The youth worker talked with the little youth group about the teenagers in the community. Some shared her excitement; others were as enthusiastic as Eeyore. But her fire wasn't dampened, and the little youth worker pressed on with her desire to do something.

"I think we can," she implored.

"I don't know..." they retorted.

She pressed on, "But I think we can."

She began to pray about it. Other youth workers joined her in praying for their small community. A few youth workers gathered once a month to pray and share ideas for an outreach. Their focus became sharper as they talked about a ministry that would reach out to all the skateboarders in their community. An event, perhaps.

The little youth worker talked with skaters every time she saw them. She began conversations with them, and she asked them questions about skating. "Is there any good place around here to skate?"

The answer was always the same: "No. No one lets us."

Her fire started burning hotter.

"I think we can! I think we can! Kids love to skate! If we simply provided them with a place to do this, we could draw a bunch of kids! We have an empty parking lot during the week. And a few carpenters who attend our church could build more ramps! I think we can!"

But then it happened.

She hit a hill.

Objections were freely unveiled. The logic of "why not" was clearly presented. Reminders about "what happened the last time we tried that!" arose. The reasons not to do it began to pile into a heap, topped off by the ultimate obstruction: "We don't want those kinds of kids around here!" Altogether it made a hill so large and steep there was no way it could be climbed.

The momentum stopped. The little youth worker felt overwhelmed. Who would have the confidence to climb such a hill of fear, doubt, and past failures?

But then her stomach started doing it again. (Darn that fast food!) She remembered the faces of all the young boys she'd met. She wanted to reach out to them. Fear and doubt pleaded with her to resist the urge to do something, but her passion was too great. She pressed on and began to climb the hill.

"I think we can!"

"But..."

"I think we can, I think we can... I really think we can!"

The skeptics were momentarily silenced. They figured she was a few fries short of a Happy Meal. But she kept right on going.

"I think we can, I think we can, I think we can..." The group of youth workers grew. Eventually other leaders in the church joined in. Funds were raised. Plans were made down to the last detail. Eventually, the little youth worker reached the top of the hill.

The skeptics finally gave up. "Fine! Just don't let them scrape their skateboards on our flowerbeds!"

"Agreed!" she said.

The outreach was a success. The boy in the blue plaid boxers and all his friends came to the first outreach event. That event sparked a weekly outreach program. Soon every Tuesday night became known as "The Parking Lot." Teenagers would come, skate, and have a good time at the church. Many started coming to Wednesday nights also, and they heard the truth about God. Soon, the town knew this church as "The Parking Lot Church."

And "the little youth leader that could" lived happily ever after.

WHERE DO WE GO FROM HERE?

You've seen the planning process throughout this book, but maybe you're still a little shaky on where to start.

You're not alone.

Try this: Start by building relationships with other youth workers in your community, town, or city. It might start with just one other person. Call and invite him to coffee. You don't need an agenda for this meeting, just get to know the person. Share with him your desire to reach out.

Ask him if you can meet again. After a few meetings, see if both of you can bring another youth worker to the meeting. Begin to share your passion with each other and pray together. This might take time. Don't rush it.

Eventually, begin praying about the possibility of doing something. Maybe it's not a citywide event. Maybe it's a campus program or a small weekly program in each of your churches. Who knows? Pray and see what God lays on your heart to do. Pray with others and see what God lays on their hearts as well. But start by building relationships and owning this passion together.

Before you know it, you'll look at the outline that appears numerous times in this book, and you'll say to yourself, "Hey, I'm already doing step number one!"

1. Pray: Give this program or event to God and bring him into the planning process at the beginning so it's his program, not your program.

2. Plan Your Purpose: Know the goal of your program or event. What end result are you shooting for? If this is an outreach program, then your goal will be to reach out to those who don't know Jesus and point them toward him. Everything you do with this program must help you achieve this goal.

3. Pinpoint Your Target Audience: Determine who you want to draw to this program. With outreach programs, remember you're drawing those who don't know Jesus, but also consider what age you'll target, what region, and maybe even more specifics.

4. Brainstorm Your Draw: What will bring your target students to this program or event? Your purpose isn't enough. You need to get them there.

5. Consider Your Resources: You need to consider your budget, your need for supplies and workers, and a plan for advertising. This step really helps you dive into the specifics of your program or event, evaluating what's feasible and what's just wishful thinking. It also provides you with rough budgets, supply lists, and worker lists.

6. Plan Your Program Agenda: Actually plan out "what happens when." This is where you put all your planning into a precise format that's going to be the most effective for achieving your purpose.

But all this starts with one phone call—one invitation to coffee.

Why aren't you dialing?

APPENDIX

Prize Solicitation Letter Sample

Dear Business Owner or Manager:

Each year, nearly 60,000 people in the United States die in car crashes as a result of drinking and driving.* Hundreds of these fatalities will occur in just one night—New Year's Eve. In the days that follow, newspapers will deliver the bad news about young lives that were lost because of stupid, unsupervised decisions. If you're like me, when you read these kinds of tragic stories, you think, *What can I do?*

I want you to know that **you *can* do something to help!** Green Hills Community Church is making a difference by providing a safe place for teenagers to hang out on Monday night, December 31, 2007. We're hosting an event called "The Safe House" for hundreds of teenagers in our community. This fun New Year's Eve event is more than just food and fun activities; it also affords kids the opportunity to go somewhere out of harm's way—a great alternative to drinking, cruising, or causing trouble.

Your business can help us provide a safe New Year's Eve alternative for the teenagers in our community by **donating a prize or gift certificate for the giveaway portion of this great event.**

We'll promote your company by mentioning your generous sponsorship both during the event as well as in any literature that's written about the event in the weeks that follow. In addition, we'll display all of our sponsors' names during the event.

Green Hills Community Church is a nonprofit organization, a 501(c)(3) with Federal Tax I.D. #12-3456789. Please consider helping us with The Safe House event and make 2008 a safe year to remember for families in our community.

Sincerely,

Jim Nasium

Event Coordinator, The Safe House

* National Center for Statistics and Analysis of the National Highway Traffic Safety Administration *2005 Traffic Safety Facts Annual Report Early Edition*

Open your doors to students outside the church! Full of real-life examples, the insights of this book will inspire you to see students as Jesus sees them—with grace and compassion. The unchurched can be reached, but it starts with knowing what you're doing, and doing it with love.

Do They Run When They See You Coming?
Reaching Out to Unchurched Teenagers
Jonathan McKee

RETAIL $12.99
ISBN 0310256607

This curriculum course (based on Youth For Christ's 3Story training) offers an interactive learning experience that equips students to live and practice the 3Story way of life—a biblically based, culturally relevant form of discipleship-evangelism. With eight 50-minute training sessions, this curriculum kit is an ideal resource for teaching students how to build deep, authentic relationships with Jesus and genuine, transparent relationships with their friends.

3Story® Evangelism Training DVD Curriculum Kit
Preparing Teenagers for a Lifestyle of Evangelism

Youth for Christ

RETAIL $99.99
ISBN 0-310-27370-6